MACHINE EMBROIDERY

Lace & See-Through Techniques

MACHINE EMBROIDERY

Lace & See-Through Techniques

MOYRA McNEILL

B.T. Batsford Ltd · London

ISBN 0 7134 4485 1

Filmset by Servis Filmsetting Ltd, Manchester

Printed and bound in Great Britain by
Anchor Brendon Limited, Tiptree, Essex
for the publishers
B.T. Batsford Ltd
4 Fitzhardinge Street
London W1H 0AH

Contents

Acknowledgment

I would like to express my thanks:

to Lilian Willey, my machine embroidery tutor of long ago, who, against great odds, impregnated my mind with the potential of machine embroidery and gave me confidence in handling machines;

to all those people, students of Beckenham Adult Education Centre and many others, who have so generously allowed their work to be photographed or have supplied photographs or ideas;

to my husband for his forbearance in times of stress and his photographic advice during the preparation of this book;

to Julie Parkes and the Bernina office in London for their generous help.

1 Machine Embroidery

The aim of this book is to introduce to the beginner and the more advanced worker a series of techniques which are possible on the ordinary domestic sewing machine, so that they can make items which are individual in character, whether for purely decorative or for utilitarian purposes.

Machine embroidery is sometimes mistakenly considered a poor relation to hand embroidery but it is a quite different craft, requiring great skill in technique and artistry in design to achieve the most effective work. Aiming slavishly to reproduce hand embroidery is, in my opinion, an entirely wrong attitude in which to approach machine embroidery today. A few techniques are loosely derived from hand embroidery but are developed in different ways, and nowadays there are many techniques and effects which are applicable only to the machine.

Many techniques can be achieved with the machine set up as for normal sewing, but others require the machine to be used 'freely', that is, with the foot removed, the feed dog lowered or covered, and the fabric probably mounted in a round frame. The advantage of free machining is that the fabric may be moved in any direction: forwards, backwards, sideways, diagonally or in tight curves.

Misconceptions arise about machine embroidery largely because it is associated in people's minds with the decoration seen on clothing in the multiple stores; it is not always realized that machine embroidery can be as individual as any other piece of work by a designer/craftsman.

Machine embroidery is also confused with the automatic patterns which are inherent in many sewing machines; while these can be used attractively and imaginatively, they are not the be-all and end-all of machine embroidery techniques. A remark heard frequently at exhibitions is: 'I would love to try this machine embroidery but my [old] machine won't do it', which indicates how well the advertisements for new machines have succeeded! The confusion lies in the belief that the machine rather than the individual produces embroidery; the sewing machine is a tool and, as with any other tool, the worker requires practice to become proficient and to develop its full potential. Perhaps one crumb of comfort is that inexpertly worked free-machine embroidery can often be more texturally interesting than superbly executed examples.

Will my machine be suitable for machine embroidery?

This question and 'which is the best sewing machine?' are the most frequently asked. Selecting a sewing machine is very like choosing a car: it has to suit personal needs. If you are buying a new machine, the questions that need to be decided before going to the showroom are:

- What do I want it to do? For example, mainly machine embroidery or dress making?
- How much have I to spend?
- How much am I going to use it?

Do not buy a machine until you have tried it yourself, and try as many as you can. If you wish to do free-machine embroidery make sure the machine is capable of it: domestic machines are manufactured primarily for dress making, with free-stitch ability as a bonus; there are one or two models that are not intended to be used in this way so make sure the dealer is clear what you require. Free-stitch embroidery in this context implies the ability of the machine to sew perfectly with foot removed, feed dog down or covered, presser foot lever down, stitch length zero and material stretched tightly in a frame. If darning is mentioned as one of the machine's functions, it is likely to be possible to do free embroidery on it.

Most machine demonstrations are shown on calico which is an extremely good-tempered fabric; insist on trying, or having demonstrated, stitching on less amenable fabrics. Take with you such fabrics as georgette, different weights of synthetic jersey, satin, gaberdine, tweed etc., to test stitch quality.

Try not to be influenced by all the technical wonders that are offered on the most expensive machines; decide what you want your machine to do and search out one that will do it. While it can be fun to experiment with automatic patterns, the basic essentials for much machine embroidery are:

- An electric motor (to leave both hands free)
- Straight stitch and zigzag

A simple range of automatic stitches is useful.

When working in a frame it is easier to work on a flat-bed machine, or one which has a detachable flat extension.

Some machine embroidery techniques require the tension to be altered in the bobbin (spool) and this can be easier when the bobbin and bobbin case are removable; if the bobbin case is removable it is a good idea to buy a second one, so that one may be kept at regular tension, and the other altered as required.

To sum up, it is not necessary to buy the most expensive machine, but if you intend to use the machine mainly for embroidery the main points to look for are:

- Quality of stitch maintained on a variety of fabrics
- Ability to free stitch
- Lower tension easily adjustable
- Flat bed or surface on which to balance a frame
- Electrically driven, allowing both hands free for manipulation
- Controls easy to remember and manipulate

The sewing machine used for each piece of work illustrated is mentioned wherever possible, giving an idea of the wide range of work that can be produced on the most ordinary machine.

Learning to use a new machine

If possible, take a course on your machine from the manufacturer or his agent: while these courses are more likely to be orientated to practical uses of the machine to make clothes or household items, it will be of great help in familiarizing yourself with the different functions of the machine and will give you confidence in operating it.

If this is not possible, read thoroughly the instruction booklet(s) supplied with the machine and make sure you know exactly which functions each knob or lever serves; it is

1 *A detail from 'Grid', inspired by ice and snow formations in Canada. The background is a wire mesh grid on which are superimposed squares which have been manipulated to become flowing shapes. Each square is edged with pelmet vilene and canvas, the centres being free machined in metal thread. Pfaff. Gail Harker.*

especially useful to be able to select a particular length or width of stitch, without having to think.

Get to know your machine well. It is a tool constructed of metal and nylon and does not have a temperament: the temperament belongs to the operator! Instruction booklets supplied with machines are invaluable; most now list reasons for faults occurring, such as thread breaking or missed stitches, so *read* and *follow* the instructions.

Follow also the directions for recommended sizes of thread and needle; the more recent machines often work best with the finer sewing threads (size 50) while older machines often prefer slightly bolder threads (size 40).

Get to know the main parts of your machine – where they are located and how to operate them. The most essential are (**fig. 3**):

Fly or balance wheel, linked to the shaft which operates the needle
Bobbin or spool pins (on or near the top of the machine)
Tension disc (also used for tightening and slackening thread)
Take-up lever (which pulls through enough thread for each stitch)
Presser foot lever
Foot (usually held by a screw or clip)
Feed dog (which feeds fabric through the machine under the foot)
Needle (plus screw hold for renewing)
Stitch length adjustment
Stitch width adjustment
Bobbin and case (below throat plate)

Learn also how the tension is adjusted, but alter this adjustment as little as possible, unless you are quite clear about what it does and how it

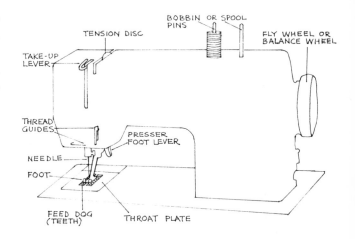

3 *Parts of the domestic sewing machine.*

does it. Most machines now have a universal tension which means that for straight stitching the tension will remain correct on differing weights of fabric. Tension adjustment is very delicate and requires *only a fraction of a turn at a time.*

Threading the machine
When faced with an unfamiliar machine the sequence for threading is:

Top: from pin, through tension disc, thread guide, take-up lever, then directly down through thread guides to the needle. If there is any minor deviation from the manufacturers' recommended route it will affect either the tension or the ability of the machine to stitch. *Bottom:* the bobbin usually unwinds so that it moves in a clockwise direction; the thread goes under a tension spring before being brought to the surface (except for special effects), otherwise the tension will be very wrong.

Maintenance of machine

Do read the machine manual carefully for advice on maintenance and follow the instructions *precisely.* When working machine embroidery the machine is often run continuously for

2 *Centre panel of 'Triptych 3': a mixture of drawn, printed and painted images on layers of silk enriched with both hand and machine embroidery. Miranda Brookes.*

long periods and in this situation some parts, for example around the bobbin case, may need oiling daily or even more frequently; but use only very small quantities of oil at a time – literally one or two drops. Machine malfunctions are often due to poor maintenance, so follow the instruction manual to the letter to avoid repair bills.

Fluff, that is minute fibres from thread or fabric, can form a 'mat' and develop in surprising amounts from prolonged machining and can be another cause of faulty running. For example, it is possible for a small pill of fluff to get stuck between the tension discs and cause a malfunction. Regularly brush out around the bobbin area and any other place where fluff can congregate.

Remember to read the manufacturers' instruction manual, which gives excellent information and advice, to ensure the smooth running of your machine. If you are in difficulty most manufacturers' main offices will be helpful in solving specific problems concerned with their machines.

Needles

It is not always realized that a variety of needle types as well as sizes are available. Most domestic sewing machines take system 130/705H (or 15 × 1). As a general rule for machine embroidery, select the thread according to the type of work and the needle size according to the thread.

Sizes
These are listed in two ranges of numbers, the ones in brackets being the older 15 × 1 sizing.

70 (9 or 10)	very fine
80 (11 or 12)	fine
90 (14)	average
100 (16)	bold for heavy fabrics
110, 120	very bold for heavy fabrics (rarely used)

These are only general guidelines; refer to your machine manual for detailed information.

Types of needles
Ballpoint needles are for any situation where piercing the threads of the fabric could cause puckering, for example synthetics and net. They are available in various sizes.

Leather needles have a three-sided point for penetrating leather easily; they are useful for dense or layered fabrics but can slice material.

Jeans needles are for heavy duty sewing as, for example, on seams on jeans.

Hemstitch or double hemstitch needles tend to pucker on the straight, but Bernina advise using them diagonally through a double layer of crisp fabric; the double hemstitch is more effective than the hemstitch and can be used on zigzag, or a simple pattern – only as wide as the foot allows, though!

Twin needles are just what their name suggests – two needles fitted into one shaft, which produce lines of parallel stitching linked to a single bobbin thread. Differing spacing is available, though the wider ones are normally the most effective for decorative work. These needles can be used in most machines but two spool pins are needed; the threads can go through the rest of the threading together. It seems unlikely to work, but it does.

Threads

The availability of threads varies from year to year and old threads disappear, while new ones are introduced.

It is not necessary to have special machine embroidery thread to do machine embroidery on a domestic sewing machine; ordinary sew-

4 *'Fish Nest' combines a variety of machine techniques including net appliqué, pulled thread, and chemical lace. Bernina and Elna.*

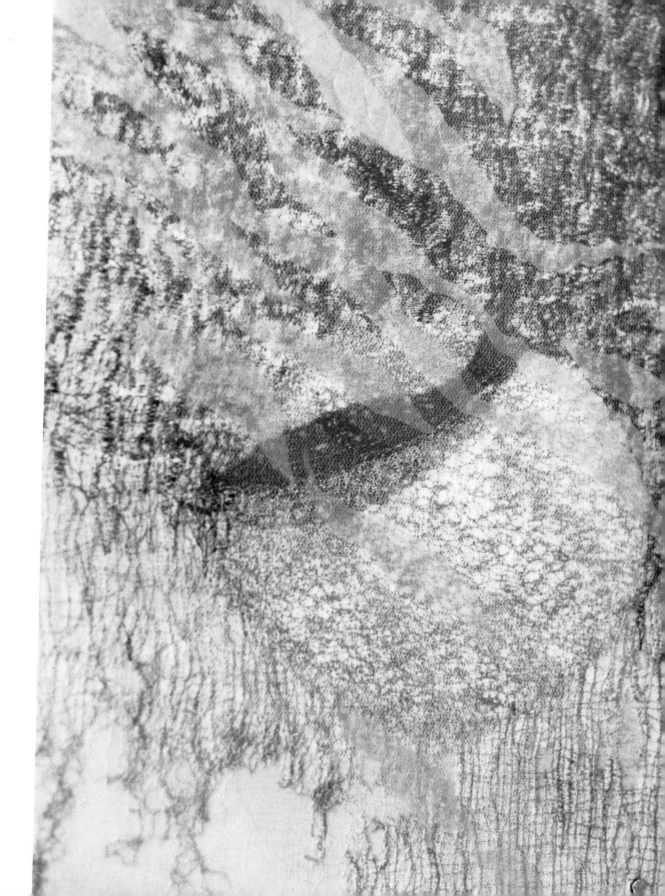

ing threads available in local shops are quite acceptable and are what the machine is designed to use.

Ordinary sewing threads are available in a wide colour spectrum, whereas it can be difficult to obtain machine embroidery threads locally, let alone in any specific colour. Nowadays sewing threads can be bought in a variety of thicknesses and types of fibre. Cotton threads usually display the size of thread thickness on the reel, from 40 (average thickness) to 50 (thinner) and 60 (thinner still but not so generally available). For most recent machines size 50 is appropriate and is a good weight for machine embroidery.

Synthetic threads vary in thickness, but by experiment many will be found suitable for embroidery and are useful where a drip-dry article is required.

Pure silk is currently available as a sewing thread and although expensive, has a texture and lustre that is unbeatable.

Buttonhole twists, sometimes called 'bold' threads, are also available and may be used for a decorative bold line of stitching in conjunction with a large needle (size 100 or 110) or in the bobbin for cable stitch.

If a large amount of thread is needed, buy a 1000-metre reel if possible, as this is considerably cheaper than ten smaller reels; these are often available from suppliers to the trade. Look out also for special offers on market stalls or end-of-range sales, especially for use in practice work.

Machine embroidery cotton is not so tightly twisted as sewing thread and is, therefore, softer. The size most commonly available is 30; just to confuse, the sizes are not the same as for sewing threads. Size 30 machine embroidery cotton is about equivalent to a 60 or 50 sewing thread. There is a size 50 machine embroidery cotton,

which is the finest machine thread I have used but it is difficult to obtain, and apparently comes in very few colours.

Rayon machine embroidery threads are now available which have a rich sheen, and are in generous-sized reels. Because vibration can make this slippery thread slide down the reel, it sometimes locks around the spool pin causing the thread to break. Machine embroiderers have developed ingenious ways of combating this, by having a special horizontal holder slightly above the machine, or by covering the spool with a thin, stretchy fabric (such as stocking or tights) with the thread emerging only at the top or side. In my experience this thread slip does depend on vibration and if this can be kept to a minimum by working on a firm surface at an even speed, there is little problem. As well as an enticing range of colours this thread also comes in multi-coloured combinations, which are most exciting to use.

Threads with a metallic finish are increasingly sold on haberdashery counters for machine embroidery as well as by specialist suppliers; follow the manufacturers' directions precisely. Even so, not all of these threads will work as described, and it is often easier to use them in the bobbin in a cable-stitch procedure.

As an experiment, it is possible to make your own vari-coloured threads. Wind some white cotton, thickness immaterial, onto an empty reel; paint on dye or ink in blotches and allow to dry. Alternatively, wind cotton thread onto an empty reel, dampen thoroughly with water, then paint on dyes or inks, and they will bleed into each other. There is no guarantee that some colours will not fade, though dyes made for cotton could be fixed by applying heat when worked. The wetness of the dye or ink will determine how far it will penetrate the wound thread, so it may be necessary to recolour when the top three or four layers of thread have been used.

Thread names

- Sewing threads:
  Drima (Coats) synthetic
  Sylko (Dewhurst) cotton
  Sylko Supreme (Dewhurst) coated cotton
  Pure Silk (Gütermanns)
  Synthetic (Gütermanns)
  Synthetic (Molnlycke)
  Cotton (Trident)
  and similar products from many other manufacturers
- Machine embroidery cotton 30: Anchor, DMC and Mettler
- Rayon machine embroidery thread: Natesh
- Metallic embroidery threads: Madeira, Gütermanns, DMC (Fil d'or) and others.

Round frames

Round frames, sometimes called tambour frames or hoops, are available for many kinds of machine embroidery and a selection of sizes is recommended to allow for differing sizes of work. Very large frames are not always a good solution as the space between the needle and the right-hand bulk of the machine, that is, under the arm of the machine, is limited, making it impossible to reach the centre of a large frame.

Three sizes which will cover most needs are: 10 cm (4 in), 15 cm (6 in) and 20 cm (8 in). Oval frames are sometimes available and can be an advantage, because they are easier to manoeuvre under the arm of the machine.

Always bind the inner ring with tape or bias binding, turning the end in and sewing it down firmly on the inside; the binding will help the frame to grip the fabric evenly and firmly (**fig. 6**).

An adjustable screw on the outer ring is necessary so that fabric can be mounted, gently tensioned, then pulled really taut before finally tightening the screw.

Round frames may be purchased in wood, metal or plastic; plastic can prove too slippery unless both rings are bound, but there is little to choose between wood and metal.

Large pieces of work

It can be difficult to deal with large pieces of work because of the limited space under the arm of the machine. The easiest way of controlling bulk is to roll or neatly fold the area(s) not being worked, and secure it with a pin, staple or paper clip at the edge; by using this method it is surprising how much the bulk can be diminished and controlled, although it does need firm manipulation to maintain accuracy in the area being worked.

Consider splitting up a large piece into areas and joining them together when completed. This can either be done in strips, squares or irregular shapes; when designing, the outlines of strips or squares could be integrated as part of the design, whereas irregular shapes are less noticeable when joined.

The space under the arm does vary from machine to machine, so this might well be a point to consider when choosing a machine.

Transferring designs

There are many ways of transferring designs which vary depending on the fabric used, and also on the availability of transfer inks, pencils and papers. But there are techniques which are standard and have been used for many years. The following are suggested alternatives for the materials likely to be used in the techniques described in this book.

Transparent or semi-opaque fabric

1 Draw the outline design boldly in black felt-tip pen on white paper.

2 Place on a flat surface, put the fabric on top and pin, weight or sellotape (scotchtape) in position.

3 Trace the design onto the fabric with any of the following:
- A very fine brush and watercolour paint
- A very finely sharpened hard pencil (leaves a permanent line; can snag delicate fabrics)

5 *A miniature gold deckchair, showing the chemical lace technique worked precisely in metal thread with areas of rich colour in the 'tree' shapes, backed with fabric.* Dorothy Walker. Embroiderers' Guild Collection.

6 *A round frame with the inner ring bound.*

● A fabric-marker felt-tip pen which should disappear when water is applied, although on some fabrics it will not do so; experiment on a spare piece of fabric first.

● A very finely sharpened crayon, the colour appropriate to the fabric, for example pale blue on white. (NB It has been found that acetone causes some crayons to bleed, tinting the thread permanently in the acetone/acetate technique.)

4 Remove weights or pins and the piece is now ready to machine.

The technique for net is described in chapter 6, page 49.

Smooth-surfaced fabric
Dressmaker's tracing paper is currently available which is water missible; it comes in several colours – white, red, green, yellow and blue in a form of 'carbon paper'.

1 Place the appropriate coloured paper face down on top of the fabric.

2 Place the design on top, preferably on a thin paper.

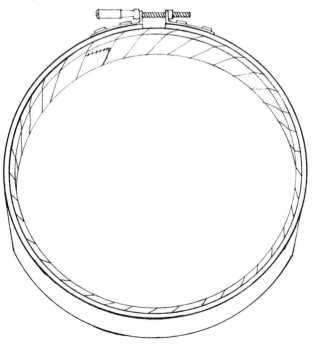

3 Secure all together with pins, drawing pins (thumb tacks), paper clips or similar at the extreme edge.

4 Using a sharp pencil, follow the design outline.

5 Before removing the design, look under one corner to ensure that the design lines show clearly on the paper.

When work is complete follow the manufacturers' instructions for removing the line.

Prick and pounce method
This is especially useful when accurate design repeats are required.

1 Trace the outline design onto tracing or greaseproof paper.

2 Turn the tracing face down on top of a soft surface such as a folded towel or sheet.

3 Using a medium sewing needle prick along the outline with holes about 1 mm ($\frac{1}{20}$ in) apart.

4 Place the fabric on a flat surface, place the tracing right side up on top of the fabric and secure with pins or weights at the outer edges.

5 Using a pounce pad, which is a tightly rolled cylinder of felt, dip one end in white powder; this can be tailor's chalk, french chalk or even talcum powder. Rub the powdered pad all round the design; do not lift or bang it but twist to and fro, keeping it flat on the paper all the time.

6 Lift a corner to check the design is complete, then remove the tracing.

7 There are now two alternatives:
(a) If the design is to be worked on quickly it may be set with a spray of methylated spirit.
(b) If a lasting design line is needed, follow the chalk outline with a fine brush and watercolour paint, allow to dry and then shake off surplus chalk.

NB If a dark line is required, charcoal powder can be used, or a mixture of charcoal powder and french chalk, making a grey powder.

2 Beginning Machine Embroidery

As mentioned in the previous chapter, a variety of threads can be used for machine embroidery, depending on the thickness and colour required. Use the same thread top and bottom, unless otherwise instructed for a specific effect.

Testing the stitch

Before beginning the actual piece always work a short length of stitching on a spare piece of the material to be used, to make sure the tension balance is correct. Correct tension is achieved when the bobbin thread is not brought to the surface nor the top pulled to the underside, but when they interlock in the fabric.

To adjust the machine for free stitching

1 Remove the foot.

2 Lower the feed dog or cover with a metal plate.

3 Set the stitch length to zero.

4 Frame the fabric tightly in a round frame, with the inner ring bound with tape (**fig. 6**). Ease the outer ring of the frame upwards a little to ensure that the inner ring and fabric rest flat on the bed of the machine. If the fabric is not taut, flat and in contact with the bed, the machine will probably not stitch properly.

Body position

This is important. Sit at the machine, place the frame under the needle and place your hands lightly either side of the ring (**fig. 9**). Consciously relax your shoulders; if your arms are at·an awkward angle, adjust the height of the seat.

Experiment with turning and manipulating the frame to and fro to get the feel. Try to develop free, fluid movements, as jerky ones can cause the thread to break or the fabric to pucker. If you are a beginner, practise running the machine unthreaded, meanwhile manipulating the frame, to gain confidence.

Starting machining

1 Place the frame under the needle.

2 *Always put the presser foot lever down now*, or the tension will be altered.

3 Bring the bobbin thread to the surface by taking one stitch manually, turning the fly wheel towards you gently. It will probably be necessary to hold the top thread lightly with the left hand to do this.

7 *Detail from 'Snow Queen Cape', inspired by ice and snow formations in Canada, and by the North American Indian use of feathers in dress decoration. Free machining has been used to form lacy fillings in open areas, lightly to secure feathers and to create texture. Pfaff. Gail Harker.*

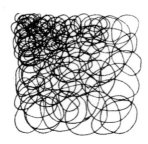

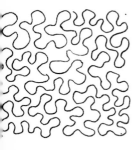

8 *Basic movements for practice when beginning machine embroidery.*

9 *The position of hands on the frame in order to control the frame movement easily.*

4 Put the needle into the fabric beside the bobbin thread, hold the two threads lightly with the left hand and machine two or three stitches on the spot. Cut off the ends close to the fabric, and this will make a secure start.

5 Now machine, going in whichever direction is required; a circular movement is the easiest for beginners (**fig. 8**).

6 To finish, take two or three stitches on the spot, and cut the top thread close to the work. Ease the frame gently from under the needle away from you, tip up and cut the bobbin thread close to fabric.

The stitch length will only be determined by the speed you move the frame – quickly for long stitches, slowly for short stitches. Do not feel rushed; even if the machine appears to be running fast, it is quite safe to move the frame slowly. Many modern machines have a choice of two speeds, and it may help to give confidence initially if the slower speed is selected. Practise controlling the frame to move in distinct directions (**fig. 8**). Moving the frame too quickly can cause the thread to break, because too much tension is put on it; or the needle can become bent, causing missed stitches.

Free stitching using the darning foot

Some machines are provided with a darning foot attachment which can be used for free stitching without the material needing to be stretched in a frame. It is important to stress that this is very much a technique which requires experimentation and the effects will vary from machine to machine. Either follow the instruction manual procedure for darning or:

1 Lower the feed dog, or cover with a plate.

2 Fit a darning foot.

3 Thread the machine normally.

4 Set the stitch length to zero.

Place the fabric under the darning foot with the fingers of each hand splayed lightly on either side to tension the fabric, and start machining (**fig. 11**).

This technique is best used when the embroiderer has had experience of working in a frame and is fully confident and conversant with the machine. Working in this way often requires a firm material, such as calico, or the fabric may need to be supported by a backing of vilene, vanishing muslin or tissue paper, or similar. This technique is particularly suitable for large pieces of work where constant mounting in a frame would be impractical.

Where a cover plate is not available and the feed dog cannot be lowered

It may still be possible to work free-machine embroidery in this situation, but you will have to experiment to find out.

Remove the foot. Set the stitch length to zero; this is particularly important as the feed dog will only move up and down and will not

10 *A tree shape made up of basic movements; it would work well on organdie or chiffon in varying weights of thread in straight stitching.*

11 *Free machining using only the darning foot; the hands are lightly tensioning the fabric.*

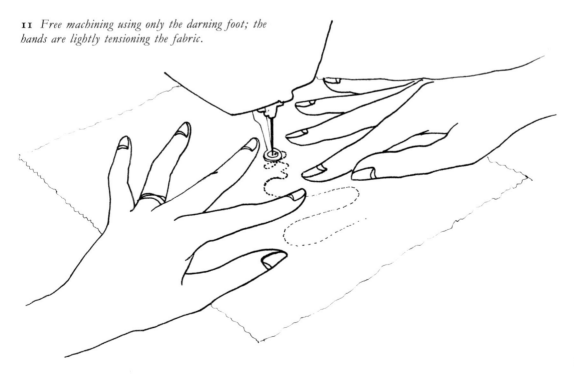

feed the material through the machine. Place the fabric in a round frame as previously described, remembering to put the presser foot lever down, and begin to machine. The fabric will probably vibrate slightly as the feed dog is underneath, but the frame may still be moved in any direction the worker wishes.

There are some delicate materials which may not be suitable for this technique as the teeth of the feed dog tend to snag the fibres; net may be one of these.

Altering the thread tension

Most recent machines have 'a universal tension' which means that the machine is designed to

12 *A daisy plant is set within a perspex box; the flowers and butterfly are worked in the acetate/acetone method in cotton thread with added snippets of fabric in the butterfly wings. The leaves are fabric and the grass is made with the tailor tacking foot. Bernina.*

sew through different weights of fabric efficiently without it being necessary to alter the tension or presser foot lever pressure. However, for specific embroidery effects it is necessary to alter the thread tension. *This must be done gently and only by minimal amounts at a time.*

The top tension is usually numbered in modern machines from 1–9, 4 or 5, for example, being normal tension. When adjusting tension

move only up or down one number at a time, consulting your machine manual as to which slackens and which tightens; if it is not already indicated it can be helpful to mark this on your machine.

On some machines where the bobbin case is a machine fixture the tension may be altered by moving round a small disc which is also numbered.

Where the bobbin case is removable it has a tension spring, controlled by a small screw. *One and a half, or at most two turns* of the screw will release the spring completely, so make *only a quarter turn* at a time (**fig. 14**). It is a good idea to buy an extra bobbin case for tension alterations.

Where a successful balance of tensions has

13 *One of a series of stones; the machine stitching is mainly in the acetate/acetone technique, mounted over an iridescent plastic which is denser in some places than others. Bernina. Mary Kay.*

been achieved for a particular effect such as whip stitch, it is worthwhile making a note of exactly how it was done, that is, the tension numbering on top, the bobbin tension, and threads used; this will save time on future occasions.

Thread colour

Usually it is assumed that top and bobbin

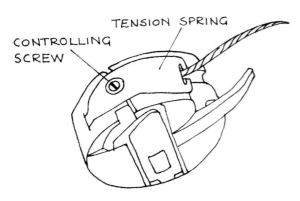

CONTROLLING SCREW

TENSION SPRING

14 *A removable bobbin case showing the tension spring and controlling screw, which slackens or tightens the tension with minimal turning.*

colour will be the same, and tensions well balanced so that the stitches are 'correct'. Nevertheless, it is possible to use different colours in top and bobbin threads to give a subtle mixture; by very slightly tightening the top thread, the bobbin thread will be brought just above the fabric surface to give a less positive line of colour, for example red on top with blue in the bobbin will give a purple tinge, or any bright colour on top with a mid grey in the bobbin will make the bright colour more subtle. As a general rule, it is wise to keep the same weight of thread, top and bottom, except for special effects.

Mixed colour effects can produce particularly interesting results for lace techniques, as back and front will be reversible but differing in colour.

Stitches

Satin stitch

The manufacturers' sewing machine manual will explain how to achieve satin stitch with the foot on, but machines vary considerably in their ability to produce an effective satin stitch. The problem is usually that when the stitch length is very short or near zero, the fabric jams under the foot, making a lumpy, ugly line. A simple

expedient is to work two bands of zigzag, one on top of the other, to get a really rich effect. The first row of stitching should be slightly narrower than the finished width and the stitch as short as is practicable; the second row is on the same stitch length but slightly wider in order to enclose the first row.

To make a very raised line a thick thread, such as pearl cotton or soft embroidery, is fed under the first row of stitching. When free machining the same technique can be followed.

Cable stitch

This is made by sewing a thick thread down with a thin one; because it is impractical to thread thick thread on top of the machine, it is wound onto the bobbin and the embroidery worked in reverse, that is, wrong side uppermost as follows:

1 Wind thick thread (pearl cotton no. 5 or no. 8, soft embroidery cotton, knitting or crochet yarns of similar weight) onto the bobbin by hand.

2 Either (a) after putting the bobbin in its case, loosen the tension plate on the bobbin case (**fig. 14**);

or (b) thread through the hole provided in the fixed casing (**fig. 15**).

15 *Thick thread bypassing tension in a fixed bobbin case for cable stitch.*

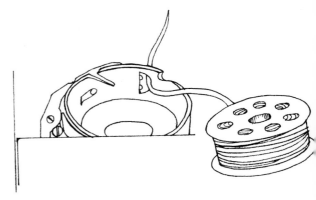

16 *Cable stitch on transparent fabric. Twilley goldfingering in bobbin; no. 50 Sylko in top threading. Bernina.*

3 Test that the thread is running freely, but remains gently tensioned, by bringing the thread up through the throat plate and pulling gently.

4 Thread the top with sewing cotton no. 40 or no. 50.

5 This stitch may be worked:
  (a) with the foot on, in which case after putting the fabric under the foot, make sure both threads are to the back before starting, to prevent snagging;
  or (b) as free embroidery; in this case move the frame reasonably quickly to prevent a build up of thread when a clear line is required, or move slowly for a knobbly, terry-towelling effect.

The threads left at start and finish can be tied off and darned in by hand for practical items. On purely decorative work the ends may be cut close to the fabric and secured if necessary with a pin point of clear adhesive.

Whip stitch

This stitch is what its name suggests: the bobbin thread whips over the top thread to make a thin, corded line.

1 Thread the bobbin with a supple thread, for example, machine embroidery cotton or rayon machine thread; slacken the tension.

2 Thread the top with a firm thread such as a no. 40 sewing thread.

3 Mount a fabric that is closely woven and has a smooth surface very tightly in a round frame; suitable fabrics are lawn, organdie, georgette, chiffon, polyester-cotton, jap silk.

4 Set the machine for free embroidery and running the machine fast, move the frame slowly.

Ideally, the bobbin thread covers the top thread in a smooth, raised sinuous line (**fig. 17**). It is tricky to get the relationship of tensions and thread just right to produce this stitch, and it should not be attempted unless the embroiderer has both patience and a clear understanding of the tension controls.

  By building up spirals of this stitch a rich encrusted surface can be created which can look like molluscs.

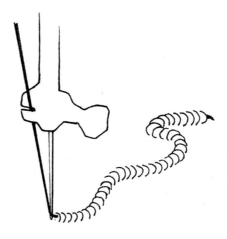

17 *Whip stitch; the size is exaggerated to show how the bobbin thread covers the top thread.*

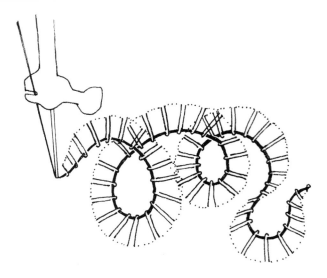

Feather stitch or spark stitch

The adjustments for this stitch are similar to those for whip stitch but need not be so precise. The differences are that the top thread is a little tighter and the frame is moved quickly in circular movements so that the stitch splays out in spokes (**fig. 18**). On transparent fabric this can be most effective as the underside of the stitch is seen as a shadow.

By experiment, a much wider range of threads can be used than for whip stitch; metallic ones can be particularly attractive and give a sparkling effect.

18 *Spark or feather stitch, exaggerated in size to show the tight top thread pulling up the bobbin thread; the dotted line indicates the shadow of the thread seen through the transparent fabric.*

19 *A stitch sampler in Titania colour-graded thread on synthetic georgette.*

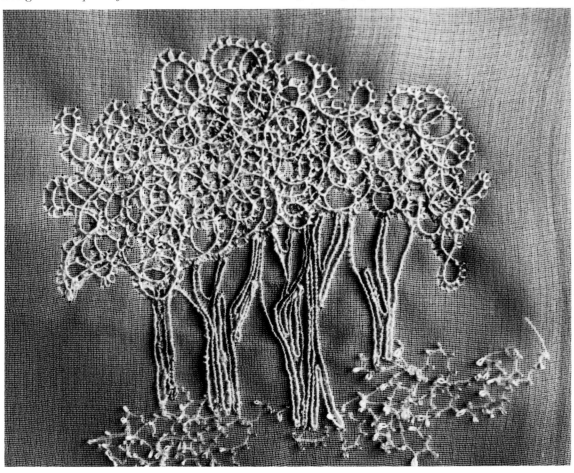

3 Chemical Lace 1: Vanishing Muslin

Vanishing muslin is a muslin chemically treated so that it crumbles when a hot iron is applied. It has two main purposes in machine embroidery: to support fabric that is floppy or thin while it is being embroidered; and to enable stitchery to be worked on it alone, so that when the muslin is vanished a tracery of stitching resembling lace remains.

Vanishing muslin is brittle and tends to rip easily, so care must be taken if it is to be mounted in a round frame. It can also be easily ripped if the machine stitching is worked jerkily; aim to develop smooth, fluid movements of the frame. Several lines of stitching worked closely together or on top of each other can cause the muslin to split as well but as it will be finally destroyed when the stitching is complete, this is not the disaster it would be on fabric.

A theory has been put forward that vanishing muslin works best, that is, crumbles, when it is 'fresh', but this is not easy to ascertain. From experience I have found that it can vary from batch to batch, some muslin crumbling easily and some not; sometimes the thickness of the embroidery can prevent the iron coming in direct contact with the muslin.

When working on vanishing muslin remember that eventually it will disappear, and, therefore, all lines of stitchery must overlap, integrate and link. If they are not interlocked the lace will fall apart, which seems obvious until it happens!

Use cotton thread when beginning on vanishing muslin so that a hot iron may be used on it without melting the thread.

To vanish vanishing muslin

When all the stitching is complete, place the work right side down on an ironing board. Heat the iron to cotton temperature, place it on the work and move it slowly to and fro. After a few seconds the muslin will turn from white to cream and then to brown, and will finally crumble; because any stitching has some thickness the areas immediately around the stitching tend to crumble last and it may be necessary to rub the whole piece between your fingers to make it fragment. If there still remain small segments of fibre gripped between stitches, pick them out with fingers or tweezers. Do not be impatient and think the muslin will disappear immediately: it can seem a long, long time.

An alternative way to destruct vanishing muslin has recently been discovered by my students: place the vanishing muslin on a baking tray or foil in a domestic oven heated to gas mark 5 (390°F) for five to six minutes, middle to top shelf. Cotton, rayon and Madeira threads seemed unaffected by the heat, and were not flattened as they are when ironed. A little rub between the fingers removed all trace of the muslin.

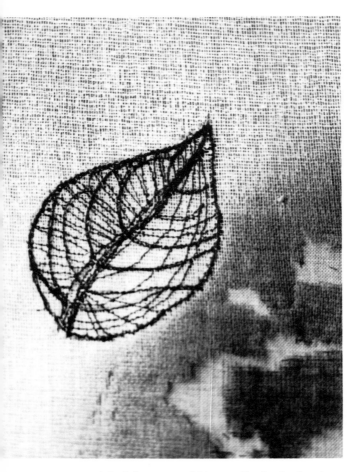

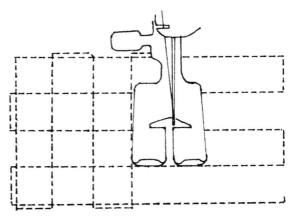

21 *A method of working a grid on vanishing muslin so that lines interlock.*

Exercise 2
To make an ogee grid move the material gently from side to side to make a wavy line and then successive wavy lines; ensure that the lines interlock (**fig. 22**), and cover with zigzag stitching if required.

If the vanishing muslin is ironed away at this stage you will have a gossamer-like open structure. To make it heavier, work more lines

22 *Alternative grids.*

20 *A leaf shape on vanishing muslin showing how heat disintegrates the muslin (lower right-hand corner).*

Learning to work on vanishing muslin

It is a good idea to work a few test pieces first to assess the technique and its possibilities; a grid can be the basis of this experiment.

Exercise 1
Stitch length 1.5 mm ($\frac{1}{16}$in.), foot on, feed dog in operation. A simple grid can be formed with the machine as for normal sewing, by machining a series of parallel lines vertically and then machining a series of parallel lines at right angles to this, in one continuous movement (**fig. 21**).

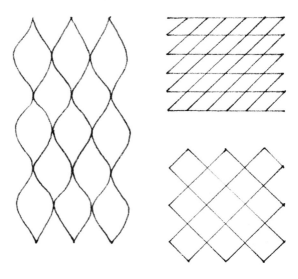

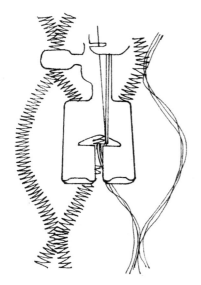

23 *An interlocked ogee grid being covered in zigzag stitching.*

work within this area. The embroidery could afterwards be used as a small mat or coaster or mounted against a contrasting background in a paperweight. A shaded machine embroidery cotton adds interest, or the top colour could be changed from time to time to give a mixed flower effect.

Having gained confidence in these basic exercises, try transferring a design directly onto the vanishing muslin (see page 15) and machine it in different weights of line formed by:

- Single lines of straight stitching.
- Multiple lines of straight stitching, remembering to interlace the lines as they are worked.
- Zigzag over multiple lines of stitching; the zigzag can be used either at a set width or altered in working from thick to thin. Zigzag tends to stiffen the final work.

over the original ones before removing the muslin, making sure they interlock and interweave. To make lines even bolder work a narrow zigzag about 2.5–3 mm ($\frac{1}{8}$ in.) wide over the existing rows of stitchery (**fig. 23**).

NB Do not try to work zigzag stitchery directly onto vanishing muslin without an underlying line of straight stitching or it will pull into a straight line when the muslin is vanished.

Free stitching on vanishing muslin

Mount the vanishing muslin with care, bearing in mind how brittle it is.

1 Slacken the screw on the round frame.

2 Place the vanishing muslin in the frame and pull taut gingerly.

3 Tighten the frame screw.

The fabric is now ready to machine, so start by working a series of circles to gain confidence (**fig. 24**)

Draw a circle, perhaps around a cup, and

24 *Beginning free stitching on vanishing muslin; work around each circle several times, interlacing lines to make a firm fabric.*

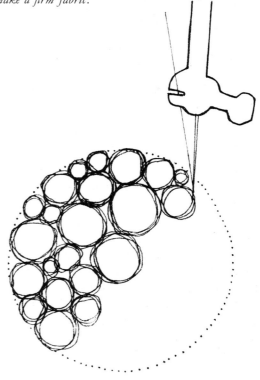

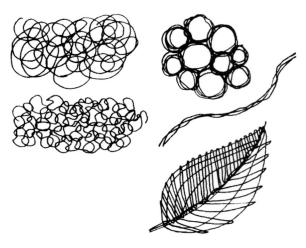

25 *Free-machined fillings showing stitching lines interlocked and overlapped so that the shape is retained when the vanishing muslin has gone.*

Fillings can also be worked (**fig. 25**). Although the resulting embroidery looks fragile and lacy it is surprisingly resilient and has been used for whole garments, notably by Robin Giddings. If the stitching is well integrated and interlocked it will launder quite successfully.

Free embroidery using the darning foot

Rather than working in a frame, especially for larger pieces, it is possible on some machines to use the darning foot (page 21). This saves having to frame the vanishing muslin, but remember to move slowly, with a reasonably fast-running machine, so that the stitches are short, to prevent drag or puckering.

Without foot or frame

Because vanishing muslin is very stiff it is sometimes possible to work entirely 'free needle'. This technique is only for the very experienced embroiderer who has both skill and confidence. Follow the directions for free embroidery, not forgetting to lower the presser foot lever. Splay the fingers of the hands, tensioning the muslin

as near to the needle as is practicable (**fig. 26**); movement may then be made in any direction. Be careful!

Non-cotton threads

It is possible, after experiment, to use non-cotton threads. Work a small area of the selected thread or yarn on vanishing muslin. Set the iron to a heat relevant to the thread, for example, rayon; by moving the iron about slowly for a much longer time than for cotton threads the muslin should still crumble. This is tedious but does mean that it is often possible to use thread differing in texture to cotton, including metal threads.

To introduce solid colour and varied texture

A recent innovation in the technique is to combine vanishing muslin with fabric pieces. In a design a denser area may be required than can be achieved by thread alone and this can be created by sewing in snippets of fabric. Cut the pieces at random into approximately 1 cm ($\frac{3}{8}$ in.) squares; there is no need to finish the edges. Pin these in position on the vanishing muslin and work lines of stitchery to connect them (**fig. 27**). Although they may fray a little when the muslin disintegrates this often enhances the textural quality.

By experiment, not only cotton fabrics may be used but also synthetic or synthetic/cotton mixes or pure silk; remember to bear in mind their fibre content when ironing off the vanishing muslin.

The embroiderer need not be limited to plain colours – patterned or colour-washed fabrics can also be used.

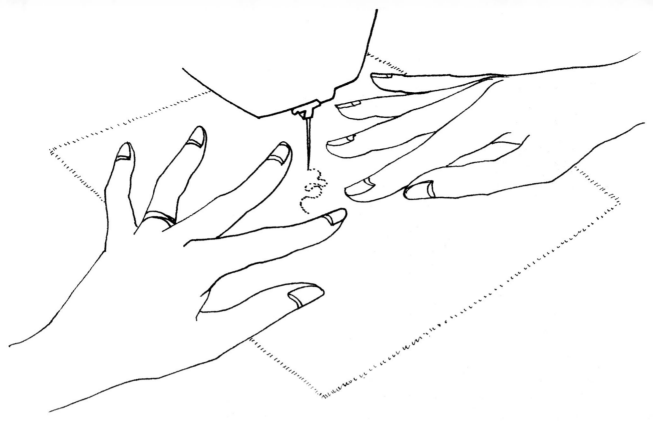

26 *Only for the very experienced and confident – hands splayed on vanishing muslin to hold it taut without a frame.*

27 *Snippets of fabric pinned onto vanishing muslin and lines of interlocked stitches being worked over them.*

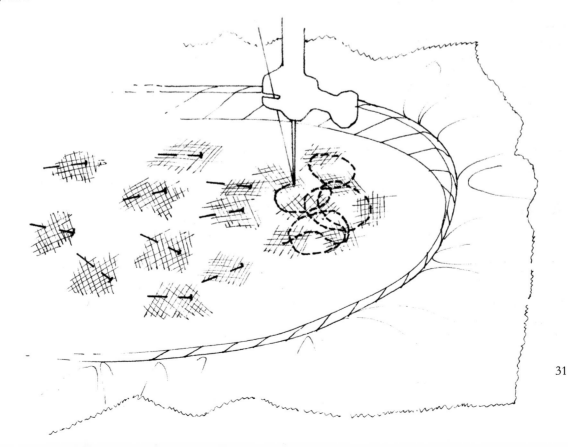

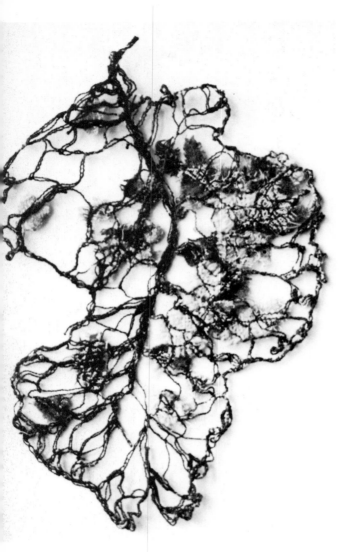

Lace edgings or inserts

Vanishing muslin is suitable for work where an area of 'lace' is required in a solid fabric. A simple application of this technique would be on a handkerchief.

Handkerchief with lace edge

1 Cut a 25 cm (10 in.) square of lawn.

2 Cut a piece of vanishing muslin 37 cm (14½ in.) square.

3 Place the lawn in the centre of the muslin and tack in position through both fabrics.

4 With the foot on, work two rows of straight stitching close together and just within the lawn edge. Trim the edge of the lawn to the stitchery. Remove tacks.

28 *A leaf skeleton worked on vanishing muslin; incorporating pieces of fabric to give density to some areas before vanishing the muslin.*

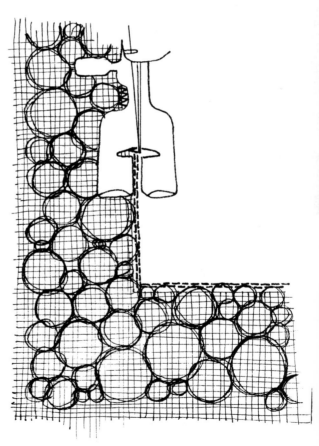

29 *The last stage of a lace edge; the circular stitching on vanishing muslin overlaps onto the raw edge of the lawn, which is being covered with zigzag stitch.*

5 Work lace on the protruding edge of the vanishing muslin in cotton thread in free embroidery, making sure it is attached to the edge of the lawn.

6 Work a close, narrow zigzag over the first two rows of straight stitching on the lawn to form a firm edge (**fig. 29**).

7 Iron away the vanishing muslin.

Using this technique, inserts or borders of lace could be made on areas of clothing such as pockets, collars and cuffs, and on many other items.

30 *A handkerchief in coffee-coloured lawn with a beige border in no. 50 sewing cotton; the border uses the basic movement of working in circles on vanishing muslin as described but the edge of the lawn is shaped rather than straight. Elna.*

4 Chemical Lace 2: Acetate/Acetone

This is a technique where the background is dissolved chemically, leaving the remaining stitchery as lace.

● *The fabric* must be pure acetate, which is often sold as a dress lining.
● *The dissolving agent* is acetone which can be obtained from chemists. Nail polish remover is *not* suitable as it contains other ingredients besides acetone.
● *Cotton thread* should be used initially as this is sure not to dissolve; but if you experiment you will find that many other threads can be used.

Although detailed exercises follow, the general sequence of work is as follows:

1 Work the design on acetate fabric ensuring that all the lines of stitchery interlock and are well integrated (see page 30). Remember that the background will not exist in the finished piece.

2 Dissolve the acetate fabric.

Always remember that acetone is a volatile and *potentially dangerous* chemical. Make sure the room is very well ventilated, or alternatively work outside in the open. Acetone is highly flammable so make sure it is stored in a properly stoppered bottle in a cool place. It must be kept away from any heat source.

Have to hand a china or glass container (cup, bowl, or jam jar), a wooden or metal knitting needle or cocktail stick and white paper towels. Dissolve the acetate fabric as follows:

1 Trim any excess fabric away from the stitching.

2 Dunk the piece in acetone, making sure it is totally immersed. Agitate with the knitting needle until the fabric dissolves; this may take several minutes. To avoid breathing in fumes, use a jam jar with a tight-fitting lid, pour acetone in, put in the piece of embroidery, close the lid and shake gently until the fabric is dissolved.

3 Remove the embroidery from the acetone with the knitting needle or stick.

4 Place the embroidery on a paper towel, ease to shape, place another paper towel on top and blot. Repeat the blotting process, with two more towels.

5 Ease the work away from the towel, pull to shape if necessary and allow to dry completely on a flat surface, which will not take long; if the embroidery is left on the paper towel it tends to stick and has paper permanently attached.

In a domestic setting, with an acetone 'bath' of limited size, it is difficult to dissolve all the acetate away completely, and the lace therefore tends to be stiff – this can be an advantage for free-standing items. After the lace has been blotted, while it is still damp, it may be quickly moulded to a shape with the fingers and then allowed to dry; it will retain its shape.

Use only sufficient acetone for the job in hand as it is not re-usable. Do not be tempted to

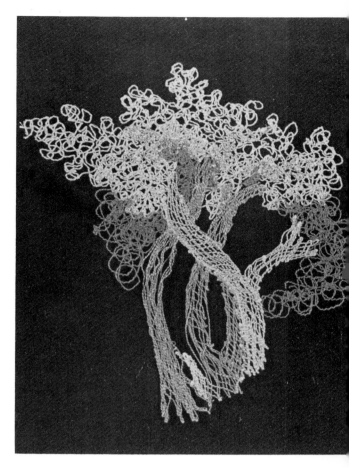

31 *Trees worked on acetate fabric before dissolving the background away. This tree was sketched very quickly while waiting in a car park, the aim being to note only the main outline.*

32 *The same design after the acetate fabric has been dissolved away. Units or motifs can be separately worked in this way and then applied to a background incorporating other motifs or techniques.*

try to rinse the lace in water when damp, as this only causes the residual acetate to congeal.

Daisy

This is a useful starting exercise for anyone who has not previously attempted this technique.

1 Mark three circles on acetate, say 3 cm, 3.5 cm and 4 cm (1¼ in., 1½ in., 1¾ in.) in diameter.

2 Within the circles work a daisy shape (**fig. 33**); do not worry if the petals vary, as the finished daisy will then look more natural.

Make sure all lines overlap or are integrated in the free embroidery. Work a different colour in the centre if desired.

3 Trim away excess fabric (**fig. 34**) and dunk in acetone as previously described (**fig. 35**).

4 When dry, layer three daisy shapes together, and sew through the centre only, by hand or machine.

The single daisy could form a dress decoration, a number of flowers could be applied to a background for a panel, or they could be grouped for a bride's or bridesmaid's head-dress.

33 *Working the daisy shape, making sure that the lines overlap so that the shape is maintained when the fabric dissolves away. Fill the centre with small circular movements.*

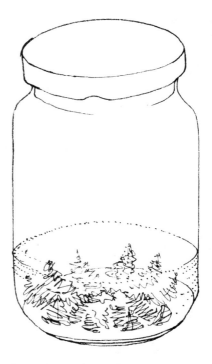

35 *A daisy submerged in sufficient acetone just to cover it. Shake the jar to encourage the dissolving process.*

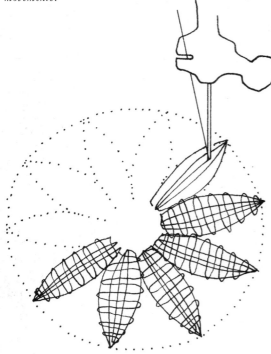

34 *Trim away the excess fabric.*

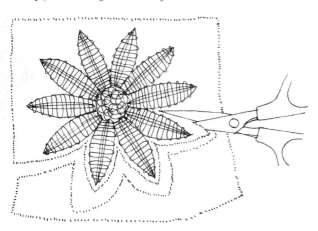

Other uses of the acetate technique

Christmas tree decorations can be formed by working snowflake shapes and incorporating a loop for hanging in the embroidery (**fig. 37**).

While this technique may generally be used for lace it also has another purpose for applied shapes on decorative work such as panels, hangings and banners. Because the work is complete in itself there is no need to turn in edges and, therefore, individual motifs can be made and later applied. Different thicknesses of thread could be combined and initials made for application to pockets or bags. One recent use of this method was for trees and small figures on a large hanging for Taberner House in Croydon; each tree consisted of several pieces, worked in varying shades of green to suggest depth. Several people were involved in doing the machine embroidery while others were able

36 *A three-layer daisy, showing how the stitching needs to be interlocked to maintain a shape. Bernina.*

37 *Christmas decorations made in the acetate/acetone technique in designs based on simple geometric forms.* Elna.

RIGHT
38 *A butterfly in chemical lace using straight stitch, zigzag and fillings to suggest wing pattern.* Bernina.

39 *A detail of a prawn, part of 'Fruits de Mer', in mixed pink and white threads and moulded around padding, with bead eyes.* Singer. Carolyn Licence.

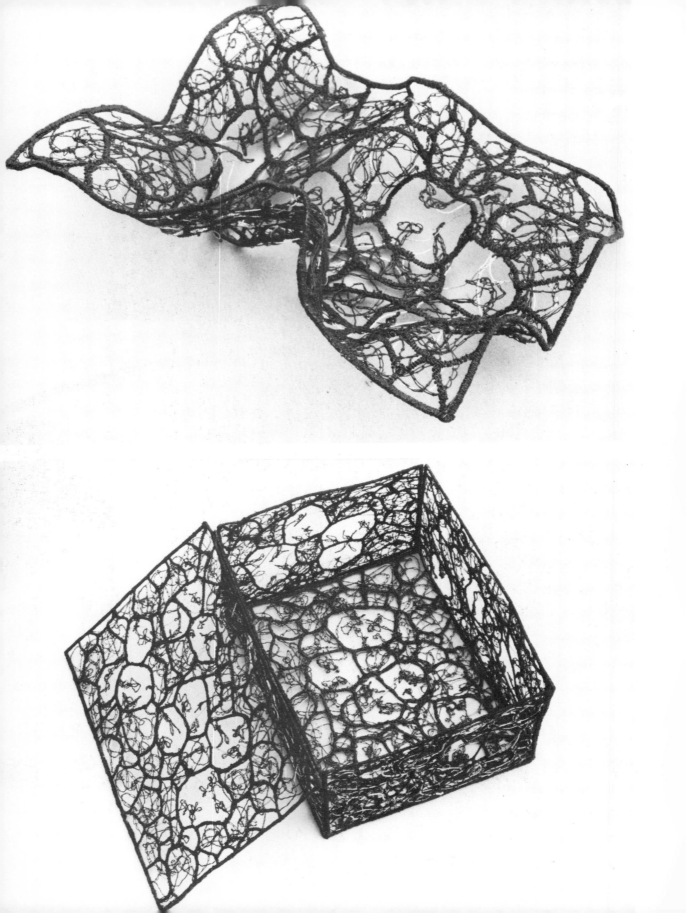

40 *A chemical lace form with a wire-stiffened edge manipulated into a free form. Singer.* Lynn Rathbone.

BELOW LEFT

41 *A see-through box made in chemical lace using a variety of threads including metal thread. Singer.* Lynn Rathbone.

42 *A representation of a wrought-iron gateway in chemical lace with side panels of covered card, forming the first layer of a multi-layered panel.* Inge Tombs.

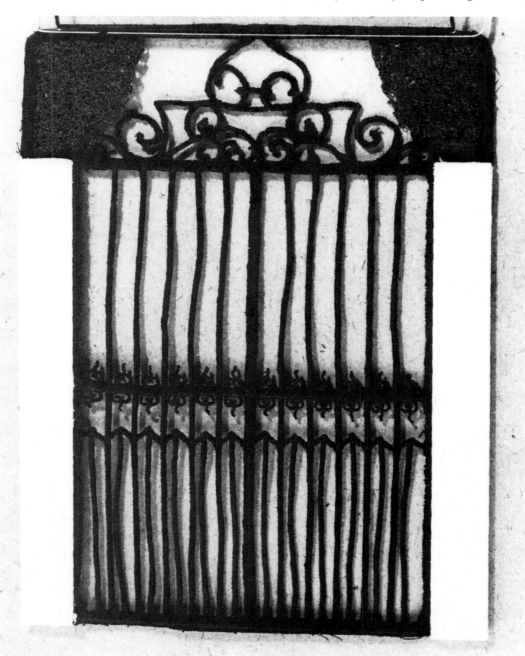

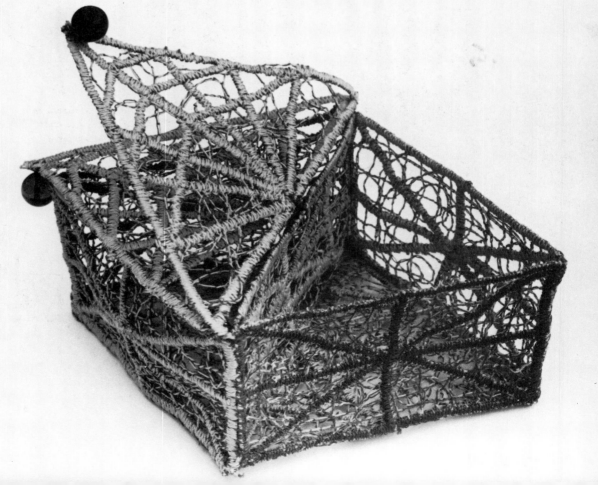

43 *Part of a skeletonized holly leaf showing a filigree pattern which could be the inspiration for lace.*
BELOW LEFT
44 *A diamond-shaped box, half yellow and half red, clearly showing the technique. Singer. Lynn Rathbone.*

45 *Monograms or names used to form earrings in chemical lace. The edges of S and ANN could be very thin wire covered with a narrow zigzag. ANN could also be repeated three or four times and the letters sewn together to form a three-dimensional triangle.*

to work on applying the pieces onto the background.

A unique form of this technique has been developed to form see-through boxes. Sections of the boxes are completed separately and the edges strengthened with wire. The sections are then sewn together to form boxes of different shapes; despite their fragile appearance they are surprisingly rigid (**fig. 41**).

By trial and error it will be found that threads other than cotton can be quite successful. To find out if it is possible to use a thread, place a length of it in acetone, leaving it for about ten minutes. Rayon thread and several metal threads seem to survive this test and so will be suitable for the technique.

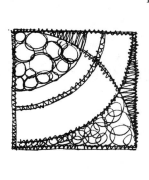
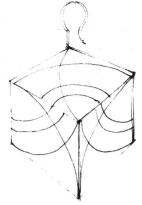

46 *A square in chemical lace, worked six times and the pieces sewn together to make a cube. On a small scale this could be an earring, slightly larger for a Christmas decoration and larger still with wire-reinforced edges to form a see-through box.*

47 *The same square in chemical lace repeated and linked to become a necklace.*

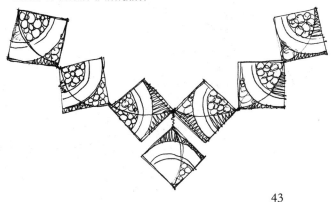

48 *A pentagon in chemical lace, which could be joined together to make an inverted flower shape or lampshade, depending on scale. If ten pentagons are joined together a 'ball' shape is formed.*

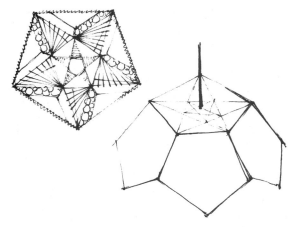

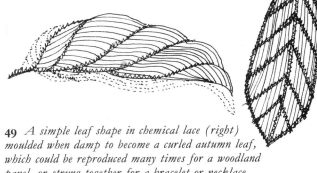

49 *A simple leaf shape in chemical lace (right) moulded when damp to become a curled autumn leaf, which could be reproduced many times for a woodland panel, or strung together for a bracelet or necklace.*

50 *'Bird in the Hand': reverse side of the pop-up card shown in colour plate 3. The bushes are made up of layered sections of chemical lace incorporating pieces of fabric; the thread is Sylko no. 50 sewing cotton. Viking/Husqvarna. Jane Walter.*

51 *A flight of butterflies, which could be used individually or grouped as decoration.*

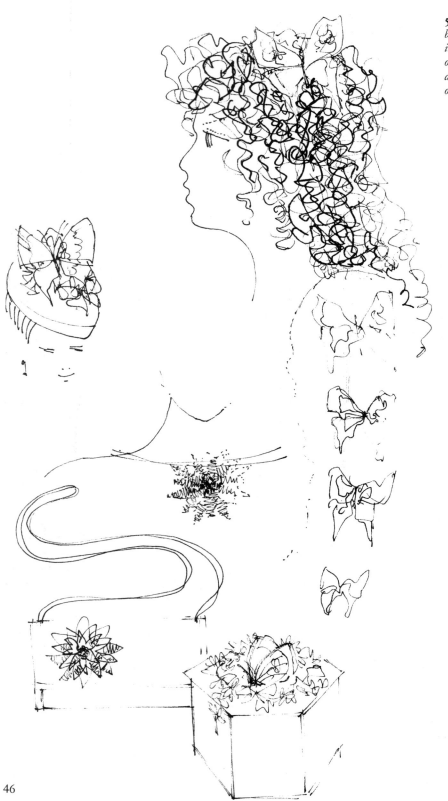

52 *Ideas for using the butterfly and daisy motifs in the hair, on a hat, bag or gift box or repeated down the sleeve of a dress or knitted top.*

5 Water-Soluble Fabric

Recently arrived on the market in the United Kingdom is a fabric that is soluble in hot water. The water-soluble fabric is fine, pale blue, closely woven, transparent and resembles organza; it seems to be not so brittle as vanishing muslin and is easily pulled taut in a round embroidery frame; provided the inner ring is bound and the adjustable screw tightened it will remain taut during the course of free machining.

The fabric can also be machined with the sewing foot in position but as it is not taut the needle tends to 'pluck' the fabric; a change to a ballpoint needle will help to cure this minor problem. As sewing machines vary in their acceptance of different techniques, experiments need to be made to determine whether it is possible to free machine with the darning foot only, which would save having to move a frame many times on a large piece of work.

I have made limited experiments with a range of threads on water-soluble fabric, including cotton sewing thread, rayon (Titania) embroidery thread, polyester sewing thread and Madeira metallic thread, all of which worked well on the fabric when free machining in a frame. If you are doubtful about the reaction to hot water of any thread it would be wise to work a test piece first, to ensure success on the main piece of work.

The techniques for working with water-soluble fabric are much the same as those used for vanishing muslin. The most important point to remember is that the fabric background will disappear and any line of stitching not connected to its neighbour will fall apart. Make sure all lines are integrated and overlapped; this does not necessarily mean close stitching – in fact, to achieve a truly lacy effect the spacing can be surprisingly bold.

When the embroidery is finished, hold it up to a strong light and you will be able to see if any lines of stitching have not connected; this can then be corrected before the fabric is dissolved.

It is a good idea to cut away any excess or spare material so that the minimum amount of fabric remains to be melted away.

To dissolve the fabric, the suppliers recommend a near boiling temperature. Keeping the embroidery opened out, place it in a generous amount of hot water. The fabric begins to dissolve by shrinking and cockling in rather an alarming way as soon as the water encloses it; ease the embroidery out gently, agitate it a little and gradually the fabric melts into the water. It does take quite a few minutes to dissolve thoroughly, even on small pieces.

I found that there were occasionally stubborn areas, for example in closely textured stitching where the fabric was slow to dissolve. One solution was to brush it gently with a soft toothbrush or rub it between the fingers. If the fabric seems particularly reluctant to dissolve, the work can be simmered gently in a pot for a minute or two and it will then certainly melt. This brief simmer does not appear to affect the thread, as cotton, rayon, polyester and metallic threads all emerge fresh and glossy.

Finally, lay the pieces out on a piece of absorbent paper, such as paper towelling, pull to shape and blot with more absorbent paper. Ease the embroidery away from the paper and allow to dry on a flat surface. It may be advisable to pin out larger pieces on fibreboard or even polystyrene to ensure that they dry to the desired shape.

It is quite possible to use water-soluble fabric when working the lace edge of a handkerchief as described on page 33, but the simmering technique is advisable to ensure that all the fabric has melted from the lawn of the handkerchief, which might otherwise be stiff.

Any new material needs time to evaluate but it would seem that this fabric may well prove an important technical advance.

Cold-water-soluble fabric

Since I began to write this book, technical developments in soluble fabrics seem to have gone ahead with exceptional speed. The latest soluble fabric available in this country resembles a fine transparent plastic, and is completely soluble in *cold* water. While care must obviously be taken to ensure that no damp touches it in storage, or it will vanish all too soon, the facility of machine embroidering on a fabric that is so easily dispersed seems to remove many of the drawbacks that chemical lace has so far presented, that is, heat or fumes.

Because this fabric dissolves so easily and leaves the thread unaltered, lace edgings for accessories or clothing might well be more readily achieved by this method than with vanishing muslin. Whole garments of 'lace' could be worked, and because the cold-water dissolution does not seem to shrink or twist the

thread as does the hot water one, it obviates the need for reshaping or pinning out.

The cold-water-soluble fabric has a close composition which seems to allow more accuracy than vanishing muslin, where lines can become distorted because of the openness and brittleness of the muslin.

To ensure that the machine stitches well, this fabric must be stretched tautly in a round frame; it may be found that the machine will skip stitches if the fabric is allowed to 'flop' or slacken in any area. In the brief time I had for experiment, a size 80 (11) needle was used in conjunction with the following threads, and all the stitching was very satisfactory:

Polyester sewing thread (Gütermanns)

Drima

Madeira metallic thread

Machine embroidery cotton 30

Titania (rayon thread)

When machining, it is probably wise to move the frame slowly while the machine is running reasonably fast, to prevent tearing the fabric.

After a brief immersion in cold water the fabric appeared to have totally disappeared, though rinsing in a second bath of water or under a running tap would probably be wise.

Transferring the design presents no problems, as the water-soluble fabric is transparent. Pin it on top of a line design, which can then be traced through with a pencil or felt-tip pen; the colour of the felt-tip pen should be considered as some colour could bleed onto the thread when it is dunked in water. Crayons do not seem to mark the surface of the fabric satisfactorily.

All in all, this seems a most promising new addition to the fabrics available to the machine embroiderer.

1 *'Greenwich Hospital': a multi-layered, see-through panel, cleverly constructed so that each panel hangs separately. The gate, trees and plants are in chemical lace.* Inge Tombs.

2 Above *'Greenwich Park': a panel based on observational drawings, interpreted using a variety of materials from net to velvet. The trees are machined net in layers. Bernina.* Rosemary Gregsten.

3 *'Bird in the Hand': an amusing pop-up card with bushes in chemical lace, layered. Viking/Husqvarna.* Jane Walter.

6 Net as a basis

Dress net has a structure of diamond or hexagonal shapes. Machining on net presents a test of skill as the fabric is delicate, but if the problems are understood from the beginning they can be easily overcome.

As net is a delicate fabric the weave may be distorted by squeezing it into a round frame already tightened; the procedure to follow is:

1 Make sure the frame is slack, with the screw nearly open.

2 Put the net in the frame gently, and pull with care to tighten the net, little by little, until it is taut.

3 Tighten the frame screw.

If the machine needle pierces the fibre of the net it tends to split so use a ballpoint needle, which enters the fabric either side of threads rather than piercing them.

When machining, move the frame slowly while running the machine fast; this will help to prevent puckering. Although puckering can be ironed out on cotton or silk nets, ironing will make no difference at all to synthetic nets, which are the most commonly available.

It is particularly important to make sure the tension is correct by working a test sample before starting as the wrong tension can be another source of puckering; you may need to slacken both top and bottom tensions a fraction.

Straight stitch is the most effective stitch on net as zigzag has no foundation to support it. By experiment it may be found that if several rows of straight stitch are worked side by side, this can support a zigzag. To vary straight stitch different thicknesses of thread can be used from no. 40 sewing thread to no. 50 machine embroidery cotton; cable stitch is also most effective.

Denser areas may be created by working straight lines close together using the weave of the net as a guide; or any of the movements shown in **fig. 8** may be developed.

Transferring the design

Trace the simplest outline of the design onto tissue paper; place this under the net and pin or tack in position. Machine with a straight stitch through the tissue and net along the outlines; tear away the paper and fill in any detail or texture by free machining.

Work on net need not be monochromatic, as a design can be embroidered in a range of colours on coloured net. Nets can be layered and then stitching worked through all layers; or alternatively each layer may be embroidered before being sandwiched, as in the trees in the 'Greenwich Park' panel (colour plate 2), to give depth.

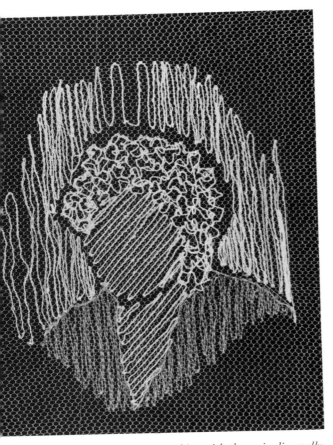

53 *Machining on net working with the grain diagonally and vertically, and a vermicelli pattern to depict hair, in a variety of threads. Elna.*

54 *Cable stitch on net: pearl cotton no. 5 in bobbin; no. 50 sewing cotton on top. Elna.*

Appliqué on net

A most effective result can be obtained when an opaque, or near opaque, fabric is applied to net, so that dense areas are next to see-through spaces; this produces a 'now-you-see-it-now-you-don't' effect.

The sequence of work is:

1 Transfer the design onto georgette or a similar fabric.

2 Place the georgette on top of the net and pin or tack in position.

3 Place in a round frame.

4 Machine around the outline of the design in straight stitch twice.

5 Remove from the frame and with great care cut away the georgette about 3 mm away from the stitching, leaving the net underneath. After the initial incision a pair of scissors with rounded tips can be used to lessen the chance of snipping the net (**fig. 57**).

Experimental work

To obtain a rich textural effect cut snippets about 1 cm by 2 cm ($\frac{3}{8}$ in. by $\frac{3}{4}$ in.) from a variety of thin materials – silks, dupions, lurex fabrics,

55 *In this design georgette was applied to net, the butterfly outlines were machined, and then areas of georgette were cut away. Elna.*

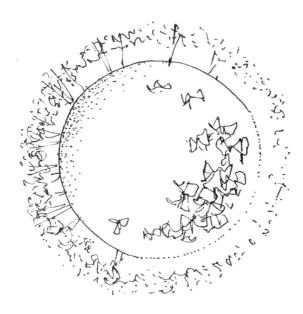

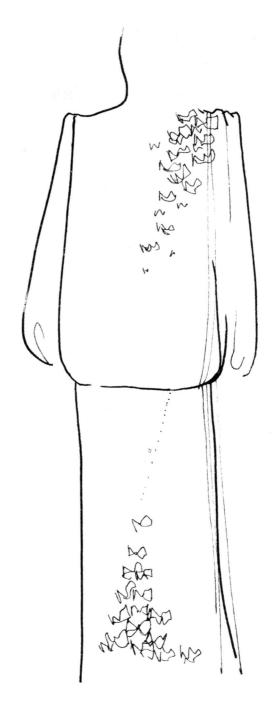

56 *Suggestions for using the design in* **fig. 55** *on a dress and a cushion.*

57 *White organdie applied to black net; the design, based on a caterpillar-eaten cabbage leaf, could be repeated in a random way on a screen or curtain.*

58 *Insect-eaten convolvulus leaves which could be a design basis for this technique; from an idea by Barbara Siedlecka.*

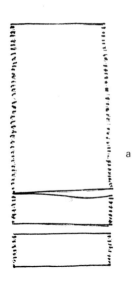

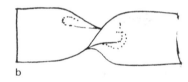

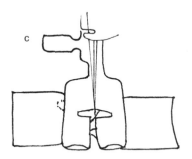

a

b

c

59 *(a) A strip of fabric torn to ensure an even width (4 cm–1½ in.); strips were then cut at right angles from it.*
(b) Twist each strip in the middle.
(c) Machine across the twist, either with the foot on as shown, or freely in a frame.
(d) The effects of tufts on net, placed at random angles.

d

fine cottons. Twist each snippet in the middle and straight stitch across the twist onto net; it will then stand away from the net at either end. These pieces of fabric can be worked closely to form a feather boa-like effect, or can be spaced or grouped to form areas of raised texture. If the embroidery is to be used for practical purposes, non-fray fabrics such as fine jerseys would be best, but in purely decorative work slightly fraying fabrics might well add to the textural richness.

Snippets of fabric may also be encapsulated between two layers of net. Straight stitch can then be worked, with the foot on or freely, across and around the snippets, either randomly or in a pattern. If the lines need to show from a design point of view, stitch in a contrasting colour, and for merging lines use fine thread to match the net in colour. Translucent snippets make this technique particularly suitable for any article displayed against light such as two-sided hangings, lampshades or curtains.

In both these techniques, because the snippets are much denser than the net, the net

background tends to disappear, so that they appear to float. This could be used to advantage to suggest movement in a panel or hanging or for fun clothing, such as a mock boa.

Wedding veil

A wedding veil might well be embroidered in any of the net techniques described or a mixture of them, but as this is very much a one-off special item, it may be helpful to follow a structured plan of campaign.

1 To determine the overall size and shape of the veil drape a piece of cheap muslin over a model and mark on it the length required, which may well vary from the front to the back.

2 Note areas in which decoration would be most effective and mark this on the muslin; it helps to have a sketched idea first to determine whether decoration is to be all over, round the hem or mainly at the back.

3 Work samples to determine technique, thickness of thread, best type of net, etc.

4 Draw the design full size.

5 Place the design underneath the net and tack only the main outlines of the design in fine coloured thread. Mark the line of the hem, but do not cut out.

6 Work the decoration and when it is complete cut off the unneeded fabric at the hem; take out tacks.

These were the stages of making the wedding veil illustrated; it was envisaged as a headdress and veil all in one with decoration in a cascade down the back. The design source was an African marigold and a series of interpretations

60 *A wedding veil in off-white pure silk net, photographed from the back, which is the viewpoint of the congregation. The aim of the design was to incorporate headdress and veil; a floral circlet lies on the top of the head with flowers cascading from it down the back. Elna.*

was worked to find the most suitable (see page 102). The net was pure silk and tended to mark however gently it was framed. The flowers were marked in tacking as circles and were then worked in free-machine straight stitch, the applied net being sewn in when this was complete, also by free machine. Last of all a line of stretch stitch, because straight stitch tended to pull, was worked round the hem, before it was trimmed. At one point the stitching snagged, pulling net and all into the bowels of the machine; it was eased out gently (not without trepidation), and a small hole had been made; in many one-off pieces this sort of disaster happens so I followed the advice 'Don't try to hide it, emphasize it': the hole became the centre of a flower and, I hope, no longer shows! (See **figs 60, 61**.)

Canvas

While taking down some net from my work-room shelf, I noticed canvas next to it, and realized that in structure the two fabrics are similar, except that one has a square grid and the other is made up of diamonds or hexagons. For canvas, treatment needed to be different, because straight stitching between the threads would have no impact. Therefore, it seemed logical to zigzag (with the foot on) over a thread or threads of the canvas.

On a canvas with 14 threads to 2.5 cm (1 in.) it is possible, by varying the zigzag width, to cover one, two or with luck three threads, so that the design can be built up with bands of stitchery following the grid of the canvas. By overlaying zigzag stitching in different colours or using colour-graded thread, it is possible to soften the rigidity of horizontal bars. It might well be effective to sew over both the horizontal and vertical bars to make a very rich grid.

Interlock canvas can be cut to shape with little risk of fraying and could, therefore, be used for box construction or manipulated surfaces (**fig. 62**).

On some pieces it might well be possible to combine both hand and machine stitchery on canvas to give textural contrasts.

61 *Detail of the veil showing machine straight stitch in no. 50 sewing cotton. The flower 'petals' are net strips cut diagonally, folded, and twisted in the middle before being stitched down over the twist with straight stitch.*

62 *'Rain over Land': machine zigzag on single thread (mono) canvas, varying the stitch length and therefore the density; The 'rain' is no. 50 sewing cotton, and the 'land' layered zigzag in Titania thread to merge colours. The top half of the panel shows canvas used diagonally which was seamed to canvas on the straight for the lower half. Bernina and Elna.*

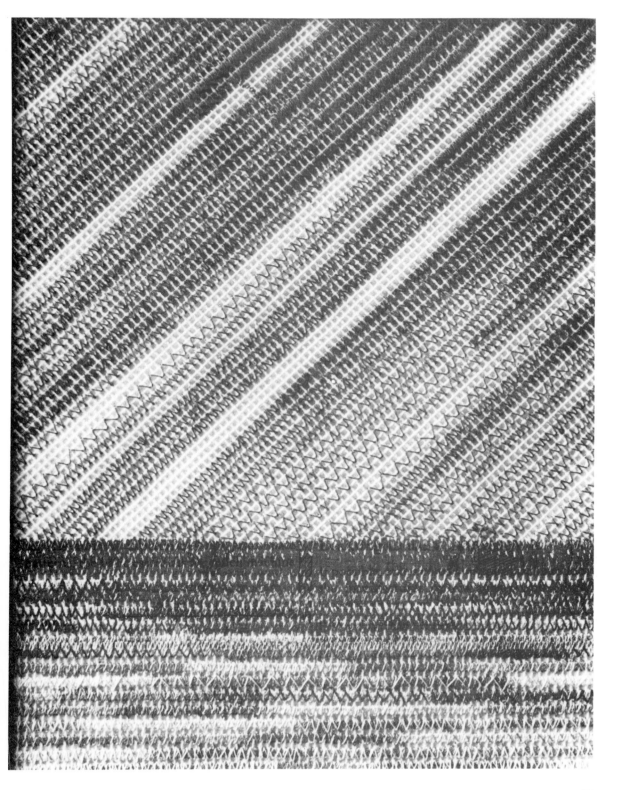

7 Layering See-Through Fabrics

There are several purposes in layering fabrics:

- To obtain colour gradations
- To achieve a range of tones
- To juxtapose contrasting textures
- To make areas denser or more transparent

A basic technique is to make a sandwich of three layers of fabric; these may be chosen from such fabrics as organza, chiffon, georgette, muslin, net and voile. Cut all the pieces the same size and pin them together all over with fine, small pins (lills) to prevent marking. Transfer the design onto the top layer and machine along the design outline; work as much stitching as is adequate to hold the layers together. Then cutting can begin either from front or back, and may be through one layer or two layers.

The basic fabrics may be varied in tone from light to dark to give depth and a three-dimensional quality. Alternatively, they can be varied in colour, for example, orange, pink, and blue-mauve, so that a range of subtle colours is developed in the layering and then the design is highlighted by revealing areas of bright colour in the cut-away areas. This technique lends itself to decorative work which can be held against light or at least spaced from the backing of the frame. Sewn more securely it could be used in fashion on a loose, flowing jacket or scarf end, as it is reversible.

Another technique is to mix threads of differing thicknesses and colours and either let them fall at random onto a piece of transparent

63 *Three layers — white chiffon, white net and black georgette — are all sewn together on the leaf outline. Areas of the top chiffon, and then the net, have been cut away. Bernina.*

64 *The ends of a pure silk chiffon scarf, with areas of double fabric, the whole being edged with whip stitch in pure silk thread. A water hyacinth was the design basis from which several interpretations emerged in embroidery. Bernina. Glenys Grimwood.*

65 *Detail of a panel entitled 'Greenwich Park', showing how the leaf area of the tree is made up of layers of machined net in a no. 50 sewing cotton. Bernina. Rosemary Gregsten.*

66 *'Snow Scene': An embroidery in the round; a differing scene or vista is revealed as one moves round it. The 'snow' base is satin with hand-quilted tracks; the trees are machine-embroidered organdie with an occasional wire in the trunk for support. Singer. Elizabeth Rowe.*

fabric or organize them into positive shapes. Place another piece of fabric on top to encapsulate them, pin at intervals all over and work machine stitching to hold them in place. More texture could be added by machining satin-stitch blocks.

Metal threads can also be encapsulated in this way and very small areas cut away to reveal occasional glints. Tinsel ribbons and Christmas braids that can look too brash on the surface can become jewel-like and mysterious under a layer of transparent fabric, with very limited pin-points allowed to show here and there through small areas of cut-away fabric.

Sewing through tinsel and lurex can blunt ordinary machine needles, so it is best to use a ballpoint needle.

OPPOSITE
67 *A layered parasol, with white poly-cotton as the base covered with white net, on which are applied leaves in white satin and cotton, with some cut-away areas within the leaves. The edge is a border of leaves in satin which is sewn to the parasol only on one edge and so stands free on the other. Frister Rossman.* Valerie Thomas.

68 *Tree group from 'Snow Scene': mainly straight stitch machining on organdie incorporating pieces of chemical lace on the leaf area. The trunks are close rows of machining, all in machine embroidery cotton no. 30.* Elizabeth Rowe.

69 *Detail of one segment of the parasol in* **fig. 67,** *showing the contrasting textures of satin, net, and cotton.*

8 Lace Based on Ribbon, Tape or Flat Braid

There are two hand embroidery techniques based on the use of tapes or ribbons which can form either a kind of lace or decorative seaming. One uses tape or ribbon bent into flowing shapes, the areas between the ribbons being filled with open stitchery to hold the ribbons to shape. The other hand technique for joining seams decoratively is based on a series of stitches, called insertion stitches, which link two tapes, ribbons or pieces of fabric with a lacy join. Both these techniques are very laborious and while it would be pointless to try to copy them precisely, the idea of linking ribbons, tapes, or even strips of fabric decoratively can be developed most satisfactorily and comparatively quickly by machine.

Basic method

1 Tack bands of ribbon onto a backing which can be either vanishing muslin, tissue paper or a recent product resembling paper, called 'stitch-and-tear'. For accuracy, lines may be drawn on the backing as a guide. Spacing between ribbons can be about 1 cm ($\frac{3}{8}$ in.).

2 Work stitching to connect the bands, which could be one of the following:
  (a) a zigzag of straight stitching (**fig 70a**)
  (b) whorls of freely worked straight stitching to form petals or circles (**fig. 70b**)
  (c) a more complex zigzag of straight stitchery (**fig. 70c**).

3 Iron off vanishing muslin or tear away paper.

This could be used as an insertion on clothing, or to make a decorative end for a scarf, for example. Automatic patterns could be adapted to make an insertion between two strips, but common sense must dictate which patterns will maintain their shape when the backing is removed.

It was found that ironing off vanishing muslin flattened ribbon and made it look over-laundered, so the following technique is an alternative.

Wide insertions

1 Tack ribbons or tapes to a backing of paper or 'stitch-and-tear', with spaces in between up 2.5 cm (1 in.).

2 Work straight stitching in a zigzag to connect the ribbons. Then work a line to connect the zigzags (**fig. 71**).

3 Remove paper.

4 Mount the resulting fabric in a frame and enrich the insertion as required with further free stitching – either straight or zigzag.

If you remove the paper at an early stage it tears away easily, and when working on the remaining threads the finished weight of stitching is easier to assess.

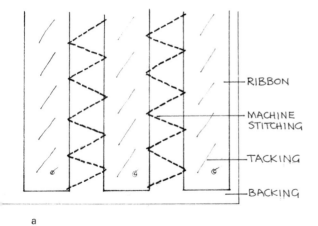

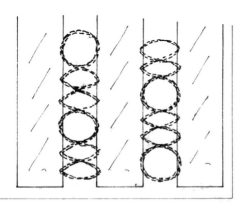

RIBBON

MACHINE STITCHING

TACKING

BACKING

a

b

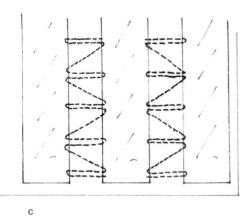

c

To construct 'lace'

Select a ribbon or braid which will bend readily.

1 Draw or trace a design based on flowing lines with as few joins as possible onto vanishing muslin.

2 Tack braid onto main outlines.

3 Machine across the spaces to form linking bars or lines, initially with straight stitching; this may later be enriched with further stitching (**fig. 73**) if required. Remember the background will vanish, so attach stitching to ribbon firmly.

4 Iron off the vanishing muslin, and lace will be left.

Experiments could be made with gold or silver ribbons or braids and metal thread in the machine, to make a dazzling lace which could be used in various dress accessories such as a bag, a cape, a bolero or a scarf. Alternatively, the braids could be coloured in pastels for a

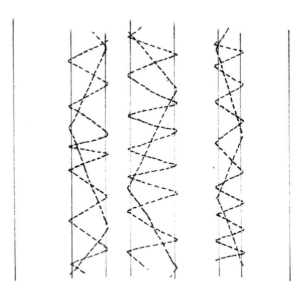

70 *Stitching to connect bands:*
(a) a zigzag of straight stitching
(b) whorls of straight stitching
(c) a more complex zigzag of straight stitching.

71 *Supporting machine lines between varying widths of ribbon, after the paper has been torn away and before the lace has been completed by adding further free stitching.*

65

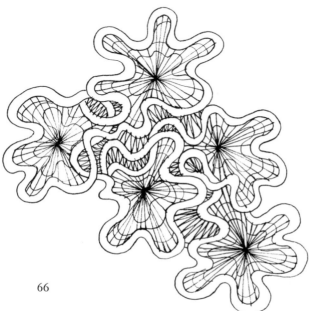

72 *Detail of a completed insertion of lace between ribbons. Bernina.*

73 *A pliable braid or ribbon could be infilled with sunray lines of straight stitching held in place by lines echoing the braid shapes to make an area of lace. Celtic designs might well form a design basis for this technique.*

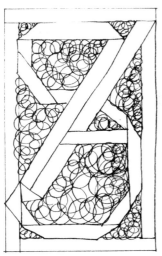

74 *The roof of The National Gallery of Art in Washington where the patterns of the blinds suggest angles which could be used as a basic structure of ribbons for hangings or shawls.*

75 *Ribbon used to form the monogram S A, infilled with free-machining in straight stitch.*

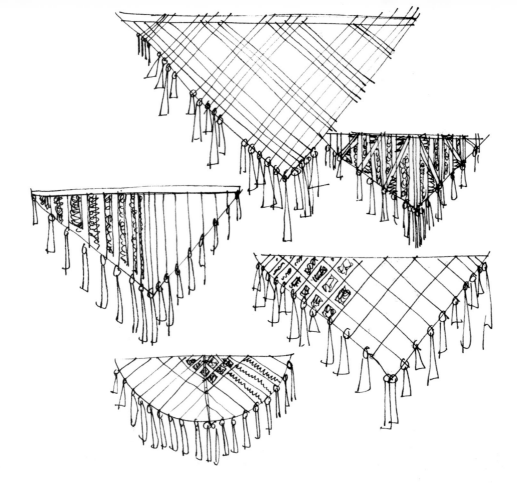

76 *A sketchbook page developing ideas for shawls or hangings based on ribbons, with machined inserts. It is much easier to clarify visual ideas by jotting them down, however sketchily, than to try to think them through.*

subtly coloured lace, or in a range of bold vibrant colours such as purple, emerald and turquoise to make a dramatic hanging.

The ribbon need not always be used flat but could be ruched or pleated, either throughout or in sections to make an area of deeper texture.

For a shawl or hanging the ground could be constructed with loosely interwoven ribbons to form a basic pattern, and then linked with stitchery as previously described (**fig. 76**). By using tapes or bindings and thread impervious to acetone it would be possible to work an acetate background: after dissolving the acetate the resultant stiffish lace could be moulded

while damp into free sculptural shapes or hair decorations.

Finishing the ends of ribbons or braids

Alternatives are:

- Zigzag stitch over the end.
- Work three rows of straight stitch side by side across the end: trim close to stitching.
- Tape lace ends can be tucked under or back, and oversewn to themselves or under an overlap.
- Nylon ribbon ends can be carefully singed with a match or candle flame to prevent fraying.
- Ends may be left hanging to form a bold fringe and either knotted to form mock tassels or the ends cut diagonally to deter fraying.

68

9 Knitting as a Basis

Knitting, whether hand or machine, can be the basic fabric on which lacy effects can be made by added machine embroidery.

77 *Machining on knitted metal thread; the knitting was purposely worked irregularly and then straight stitch in coloured threads was worked over and between the metal thread to intensify some areas. Bernina.*

Hand knitting

You will need two very large knitting needles, or one large and one smaller, and a firm yarn such as pearl cotton, crochet cotton, or even metal thread. This is very much a 'by experiment' technique, but a pattern such as the following, based on 15 stitches, will give an open random mesh.

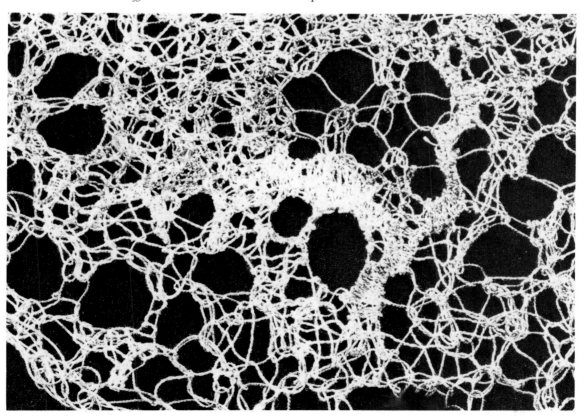

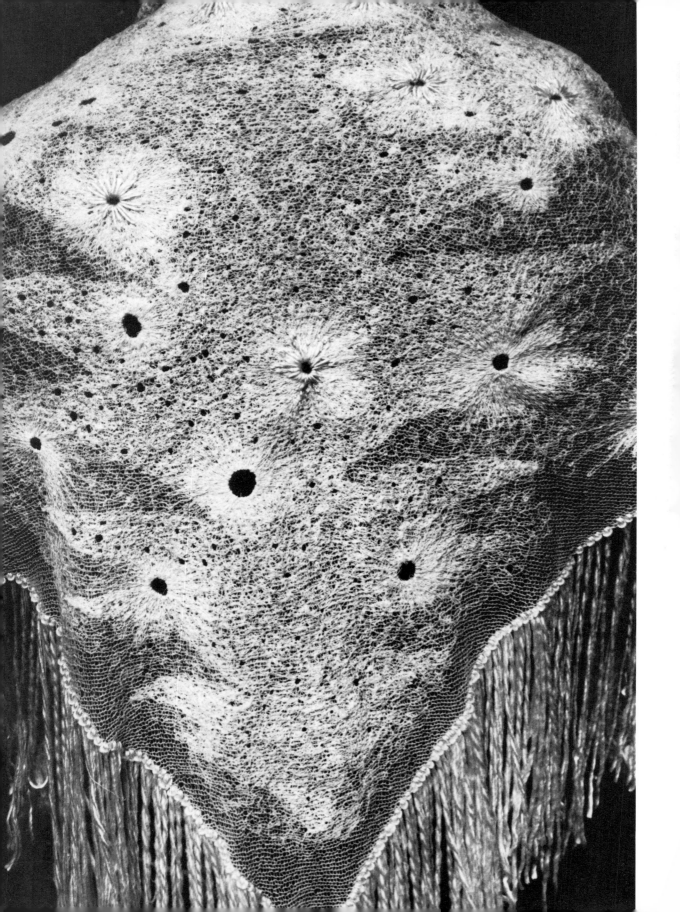

78 *A shawl in machine knitting, with machine embroidery making main textures and holes, but with a little hand embroidery in pure silk to enrich the 'flowers', and also to form the fringe. Singer (treadle). Pamela Pavitt.*

79 *Detail of the shawl, showing the machine textures on knitting.*

1st row Knit 2 tog, make 3, knit 2 tog twice, make 4, knit 4, knit 3 tog, knit 2 tog.
2nd row Purl.
3rd row As 1st row but begin half way through (for example at 'knit 4').
4th row Purl.

Cast off when sufficient has been knitted to mount in a round frame. Frame and stretch taut. Now machine over and between the knitted lines, emphasizing some of the larger holes and making a filigree in between other lines by working to and fro across the space.

Although the knitting seems floppy and insecure, by the time it has been machined into, it becomes much firmer and could be manipulated into cravats, bows or belts or, if large enough, a whole hanging.

Subtle colour variations may be made by using contrasting colours in bobbin and top, or by working with a variegated thread in bobbin and top.

Experiments could also be carried out on loosely knitted fabrics, cutting slits or holes if necessary; stockinette, as sold for washing up cloths, could form a good basis for experiment.

10 Pulled Thread by Machine

Machine textures in straight stitch are often thought of as thin or ineffective but by using the zigzag in any of its various widths much richer textures can be achieved than with straight stitch. One technique is pulled work on the machine which has a much freer look than its hand-worked counterpart. However, it is necessary to select the right kind of fabric as the balance between fabric and thread is crucial in this technique; its effectiveness relies on areas being filled rather than on linear work.

The fabric must be both loosely and openly woven so that the threads move easily: muslin will give guaranteed results though many other fabrics will be found suitable when tested, such as scrim, which can be obtained in different weights and will give bolder textures. The idea is to group the threads of the fabric together with zigzag, which can be done as follows:

1 Set the machine to free embroidery (page 18).

2 Use any sewing cotton, in both top and bobbin; tensions may need to be tightened slightly.

3 Frame the fabric very tautly in a round frame.

4 Start as usual with a few stitches on the spot; set the zigzag to full width and begin machining. Move the frame slowly so that it pulls the fabric, and also move it gently from side to side, following the line of the grain but seesawing across it. Continue succeeding rows of stitchery in the same way, butting up to the previous row to give the biggest holes.

5 If desired, other rows may then be worked on top, roughly at right angles to the first row and following the grain in that direction; this will tend to hide the fabric completely and produces a very rich textural effect.

By using a colour-shaded or multi-coloured thread the texture may be further enriched. Madeira machine embroidery metallic threads can be employed in this technique most successfully either on their own or mixed with areas of coloured threads. This rich textured fabric could form a jerkin, belt or bag or applied areas on purely decorative work.

An extension of this technique to create larger holes is to cut slits before machining.

Slit technique

1 Cut slits about 1.5 cm ($\frac{5}{8}$ in.) long on the grain of the fabric when it is already mounted in the frame (**fig. 81**); make slits in a random arrangement.

2 Work zigzag at its widest over these edges and in between the slits, moving the frame gently from side to side (**fig. 82**). This will make petal-shaped holes, the original slit dictating the final hole size.

4 'Confection': a butterfly in chemical lace on a background lightly quilted by machine, with free-standing organza leaves outlined in machine stitching. Bernina and Elna.

5 Above *A collection of soft sculpture stones in a variety of experimental machine techniques, including chemical lace. Bernina. Mary Kay.*

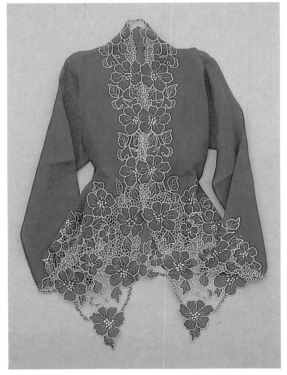

6 *A voile jacket by Chong Pat Moye to be worn over a sarong. The embroidery was worked on a Singer treadle machine, probably about 20 years ago. This is only one of a collection of jackets all designed and worked by the same artist and all equally attractive.*

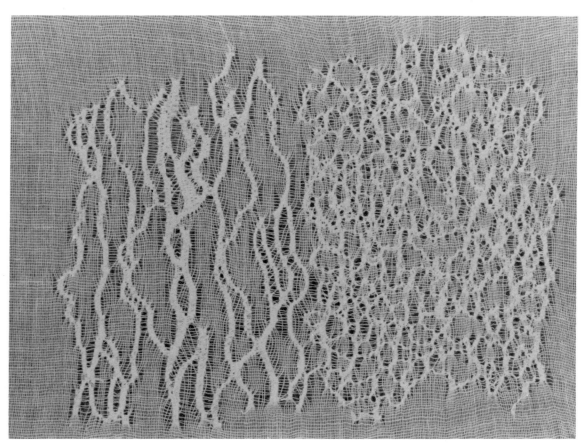

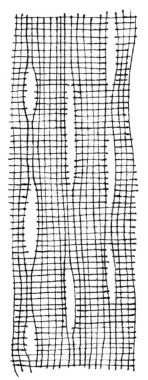

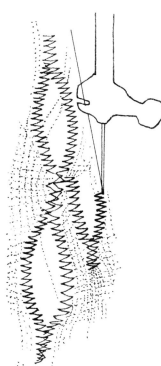

80 *Textures on muslin. Left: machine set on zigzag and fabric moved from side to side; right: machine set at full width zigzag and stitching worked in a vermicelli pattern. Elna.*

81 *Slits cut on the grain of openweave fabric.*

82 *Pulling slits into leaf shapes with zigzag stitch set at full width.*

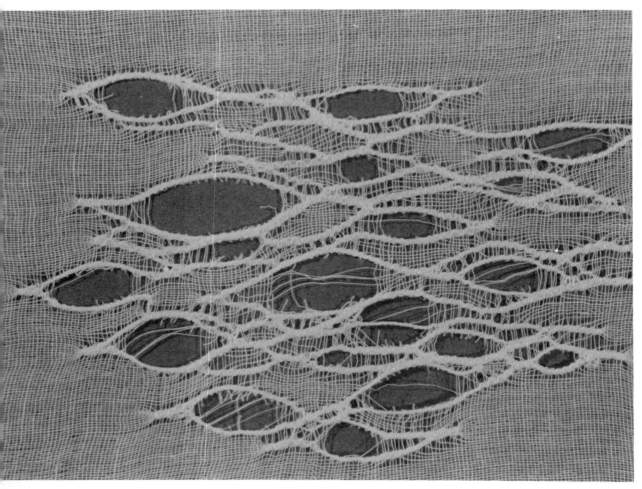

83 *Slits cut in fabric and then zigzag-machined; no. 50 sewing cotton on muslin. Elna.*

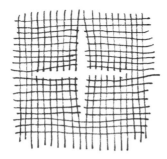

84 *A cross cut on the grain of the fabric.*

RIGHT
85 *Machining outwards from the cross to make a circle.*

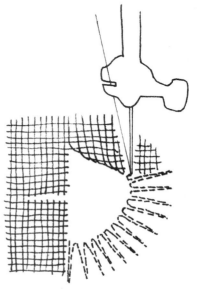

Circular hole technique

1 Cut two slits at right angles, that is, in a cross (**fig. 84**), once the fabric is framed.

2 Now work straight-stitch lines, from the centre outwards and back again (**fig. 85**); this will pull the fabric back into a round hole. A group of these holes makes a bold texture.

NB Cut the slits in either of these techniques much smaller than the required final size as they enlarge considerably in the working.

Experiments can be made with slits on the diagonal so that the fabric stretches and wrinkles.

86 *Cross slits become circles on muslin or similar fabric. Bernina.*

87 *A leaf combining pulled thread textures and holes on muslin.*

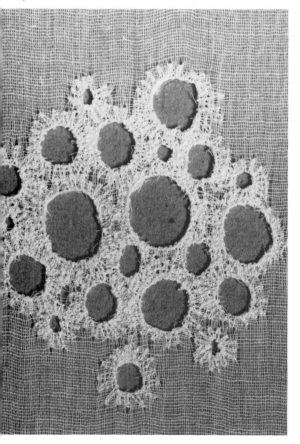

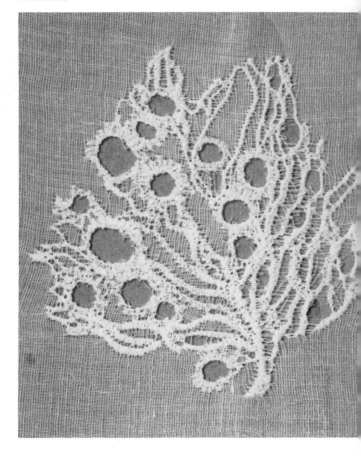

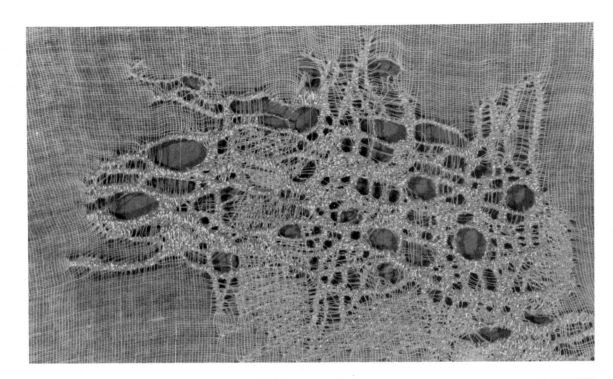

76

88 *Slits cut in fabric and the lines of full width zigzag worked both vertically and horizontally in Madeira thread, with no. 50 sewing cotton in the bobbin.* Elna.

89 *Evenweave linen with threads removed both horizontally and vertically in a random check pattern; zigzag stitch is then worked over the remaining threads in both directions; no. 40 sewing cotton.* Bernina.

ABOVE

90 *'Onion': the outer surface is pulled thread machine stitching on scrim and is mounted over a gold lurex fabric; the ends of the scrim have been allowed to fray to represent the dried leaves and roots.* Pamela Warner.

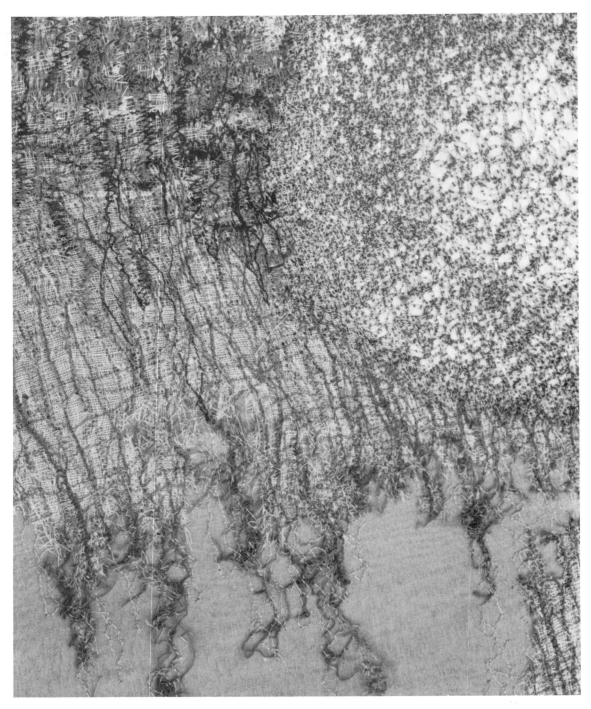

91 *Detail of 'Fish Nest' illustrating the textured background worked on vanishing muslin and muslin, in ombre machine embroidery cotton and no. 50 sewing cotton. Two shades of machine embroidery cotton were used, one on the top threading and one in the bobbin, to give the area within the circle its speckly effect. Bernina and Elna.*

11 Cutwork

Cutwork in hand embroidery is usually associated with a specific weight of fabric and thread; while the machine technique follows the stages of construction of the hand technique it is much more flexible in its fabric requirements and can be worked on fabrics as diverse as silk, crepe de chine and gaberdine. For machine cutwork a good close satin stitch is preferable, so to ensure success it is worth experimenting first on the fabric to be used.

Follow the instructions in your machine manual for satin stitch; depending on the make, some machines will allow the stitch length to be almost zero and others require a little more stitch length to allow the feed dog to operate and to avoid the fabric jamming under the foot. A recent innovation is for some machines to be provided with a foot with a channel cut in its underside specifically for satin stitch.

Corners can be a problem, as if one row of stitching overlaps another, jamming can occur. Try to avoid this by working one side beyond the corner and starting the next corner at right angles to it (**fig. 93**).

When beginning this technique use a firm, closely woven fabric, for example, calico, poplin or poly-cotton, and threads that match in colour. Contrasting colour thread will accentuate a less than perfect satin stitch. By experiment, many other fabrics can be used from crepe de chine, lawn and satin to fine wools, gaberdine and even needlecord and jersey.

To support flimsy materials such as lawn, fine jersey and crepe de chine, use a stiff paper-like backing ('stitch-and-tear') which can be torn off when stitching is complete. Pin or tack it onto the back of the fabric before commencing the cutwork. Alternatively, vanishing muslin may be used to support the fabric; but where a hot iron cannot be used, for example with synthetic fabrics, removing it may be a tedious process.

Designing

When designing for cutwork, remember that if the area cut away is too large the fabric will sag or stretch out of shape; or if one area does not link with its neighbour the whole piece can fall apart! To prevent this disappointment, draw the design on paper and then actually cut out the areas of holes; any errors will soon be evident, and may be corrected before the design is worked on fabric.

Basic method 1

Use the machine with the ordinary sewing foot in position and the feed dog in operation. Work on a closely woven, medium-weight fabric such as calico or poplin, with thread of a matching colour. Transfer the design onto the fabric, and tack to a backing (vanishing muslin or 'stitch-and-tear').

1 Set the stitch length to 2 mm ($\frac{1}{16}$ in.) and work two rows of straight stitch side by side around

92 *'Window Scene': the net curtains are a free form of cutwork combining hand and machine techniques, backed with coloured paper and fabric, on which are superimposed the table and vase. Elna.* Margaret Gartell.

80

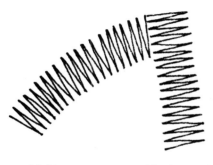

93 *Making a neat corner with zigzag stitch.*

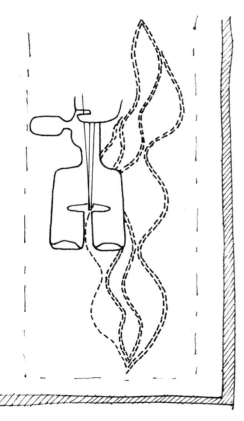

94 *Two lines of straight stitch being worked along the outline through fabric and backing.*

the outline of the design (**fig. 94**). This stitching acts as stay stitching and the backing will prevent the edge stretching when areas of fabric are cut away. Remove the tacking.

2 When the whole design has been straight stitched cut away the required areas of fabric (**fig. 95**) but not the backing.

3 Set the machine to satin stitch, about 3–4 mm ($\frac{1}{4}$ in.) wide, and machine over the two rows of straight stitch and the edge of the fabric (**fig. 96**). Let the needle just go over the edge on one side. The advantage of this technique is that the zigzag stitching encloses the frayed edges, giving a neat finish. Finally, remove the backing.

If a more raised edge is desired, either work a second row of satin stitch, wider than the first, over it, or place a 'cord', perhaps of pearl cotton no. 5 or soft embroidery thread, under the satin stitch as it is worked. Some machines, such as Bernina, have a foot with a small hole in it, through which the cord is threaded to feed under the satin stitch.

95 *Cut away the material where the holes are to be, but leave the backing.*

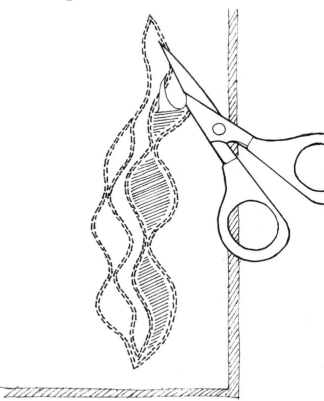

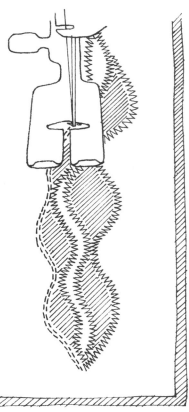

Basic method 2

1 As 1 in previous method.

2 Work satin stitch over the rows of straight stitching. Remove the backing.

3 Cut away open areas with a very sharp pair of scissors, as close to the stitching as possible. With this method it is almost impossible to cut so close to the stitchery that no frayed edge remains. By machining with matching thread, this is far less obvious than threads of a strongly contrasting colour (for example mid blue on white).

These techniques can also be adopted on other fabrics such as crepe de chine, wool or synthetic crepe, and jerseys of differing weights.

96 *Zigzag over the edge to neaten. When complete tear away the backing.*

97 *A child's cutwork collar in fine white lawn, in a repeat pattern based on a butterfly. Elna.*

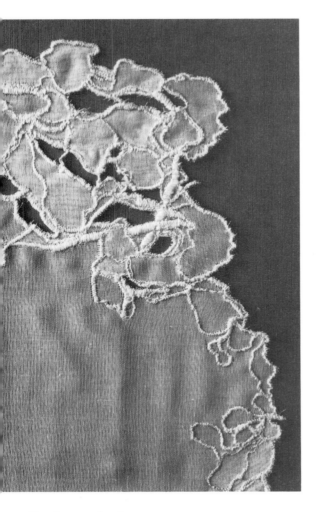

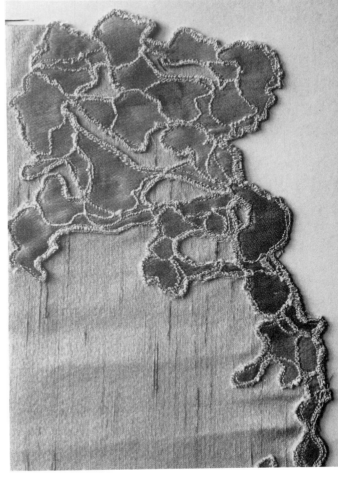

Basic method 3

Before commencing, cover the back of the work entirely with an iron-on interfacing such as vilene or Staflex. Make sure the interfacing adheres thoroughly all over the fabric, before beginning the cutwork. Now follow instructions for method 1, but without the backing. Some iron-on interfacings alter the fabric: it has been found, for example, that pure silk wrinkles. It would therefore be advisable to carry out tests on a small piece before going ahead with a major piece of work. The final result of this technique is a fabric less supple than that produced by the two previous methods but one which enables holes to be cut larger and still

98 *A cutwork edging worked on cotton voile in no. 60 sewing cotton. Bernina.* Glenys Grimwood.

99 *The same design, based on a water hyacinth, worked in a different cutwork technique. Satin was coloured with inks to give a pastel flowery look and applied to a neutral-coloured rayon dupion; after stitching the two together, areas were cut away, leaving a satin edging to the dupion. Bernina.* Glenys Grimwood.

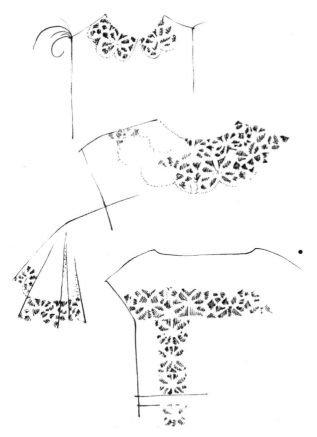

in a frame or darning foot only, and unbacked. In this way more elaborate shapes and curves can be managed than with the foot on; the zigzag is set to a specific width and its density depends on the speed at which the frame is moved.

By operating the knob or lever controlling the zigzag width with one hand and moving the frame with the other, the edging can be varied in width, which gives a pleasing quality of line.

It would also be interesting to experiment with automatic patterns to finish the edges.

Alternative method 4

This technique is useful for hangings or blinds as it is stiff, but could also be adapted to lampshades (**fig. 102**). It also means that larger holes can be cut as the fabric is well supported.

100 *Ideas to show how the border in the child's cutwork collar (***fig. 97***) could be adapted to other clothes.*

101 *An experimental cutwork piece using cotton poplin bonded to pelmet vilene; the design is based on an iron bracket seen on Witham station. By supporting the fabric in this way, much larger areas can be cut away without it sagging. Elna.*

maintain their shape. It is probably more applicable to purely decorative work than to utilitarian items. It has the advantage of preventing fabrics fraying so that it enlarges the scope of types of fabric to be used.

An alternative experiment would be to bond two different fabrics together with Bondaweb (a paper-backed adhesive), before commencing cutwork so that the completed piece is reversible with a different colour and/or texture on either side.

So far the cutwork techniques have suggested using the foot on, but there is no reason why the same technique should not be developed using a free needle, with fabric mounted

102 *Suggestions for adapting cutwork method 4 for use on lampshades.*

103 *Cut paper borders and motifs. These are from a series of visual aids made by Barbara Siedlecka which were suggested by traditional Polish paper cutting. They could be readily adapted to cutwork or appliqué on net.*

1 Transfer the design onto fabric – cotton poplin for example.

2 Iron Bondaweb onto the back of the fabric.

3 Remove the Bondaweb paper backing and iron a stiff backing, such as pelmet vilene, onto the poplin. Make sure the poplin is bonded securely all over. On large pieces iron systematically from the centre outwards to avoid wrinkles.

4 Work a single line of straight stitch with the foot on or not, as the design shapes dictate.

5 Cut away areas of holes through all layers, as close to the stitching as possible, about 1 mm ($\frac{1}{20}$ in.).

6 Work satin stitch over all edges.

104 *Detail of a hanging worked in the technique described, but with the addition of machine-applied snippets of coloured lurex fabric. The backing is also colour-sprayed and decorated with machine appliqué. Bernina and Elna.*

Experimental cutwork

All the previous methods in this chapter have assumed that a flat unwrinkled finish is the final aim, but experiments with cutwork can produce a corrugated edge making an attractive alternative, or the edges could be only lightly zigzagged and purposely frayed.

To obtain a corrugated edge cut slits on the cross and zigzag over the edge without any stay stitching. If possible, pull the material as it feeds through the machine to emphasize the stretch.

To fray the edge, work an open zigzag around the shape, cut a slit through the middle of the hole and fray out the fabric to the stitching.

105 *Slits cut on the cross grain and edges closely zigzagged to make them wrinkle and stretch.*

106 *Slits cut on the cross grain; a leaf shape worked in open zigzag round them; the fabric is then frayed out from the slit to the stitching.*

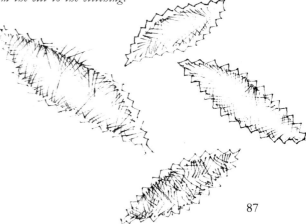

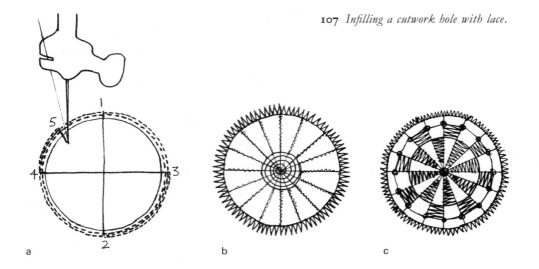

a   b   c

Cutwork with lace fillings

An extension of cutwork perfected by Dorothy Benson in the late 1930s and shown in her book *Machine Embroidery* was infilling the cutwork hole with lace. It may not always be realized, even by machine embroiderers, that it is possible to machine across space as long as the machining is anchored on some material at either side. This allows a web of machined lines to be made.

The procedure is as follows:

1 Frame up tightly a piece of closely woven fabric, such as lawn, organdie, poplin, calico. Set the machine for free embroidery.

2 Work two lines of straight stitching close together around the outline of the shape, in this instance a circle.

3 Cut out the centre of the shape quite close to the stitching.

4 Continuing with straight stitch, make a firm start with several stitches on the spot, then machine across to the other side moving smoothly and unhurriedly; attach to the other edge with two or three stitches. The top and bobbin threads will twist together. Make as

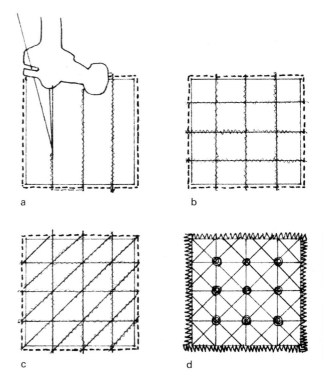

a   b

c   d

108 *Dorothy Benson invented a lace filling for squares, and the sequence of work is shown from a to d; aim to keep the sides of the square on the grain of the material to prevent uneven edges.*

many lines or spokes as required (**fig. 107a, b**). Machine more solid areas into this structure by working from spoke to spoke and back again (**fig. 107c**), if a richer filling is required.

5 Lastly, finish off the edge, by either zigzagging over it or straight stitching in a similar manner to that shown in fig. 89.

109 *Detail of the edge of a jacket worked by Chong Pat Moye in Malaysia about 20 years ago. This delightful embroidery was produced on a Singer treadle machine without zigzag; the satin stitch was made by moving the frame to and fro rhythmically as described in Dorothy Benson's book* Machine Embroidery, *but considerable skill and practice is needed to produce work as technically perfect as this. White thread has been used on dark green robbia voile.*

110 *Another detail of a jacket by Chong Pat Moye which is a form of extended cutwork; the embroidery is* *worked in ombre thread, white to orange on a dull orange robbia voile. Singer (treadle).*

12 Plastic or Paper as a Basis

Working on plastic or paper is a recent development and experimental pieces can be seen in current exhibitions by a number of modern embroiderers.

III *Detail of a hanging made in paper, varnished and in some places also marbled, which was then pleated and tucked by machine. The colours used are browns, terracotta and beige. Singer. Rosalie Bygrave.*

Paper

Varnishing tissue paper or typing paper tends to make it translucent and the varnish also seems to add flexibility. Many of the techniques already mentioned can be applied to papers, such as layering, cutwork, joining strips decoratively and working 'lace' fillings in a frame of paper.

Home-made paper tends to be thicker and less dense in texture so holes can be purposely

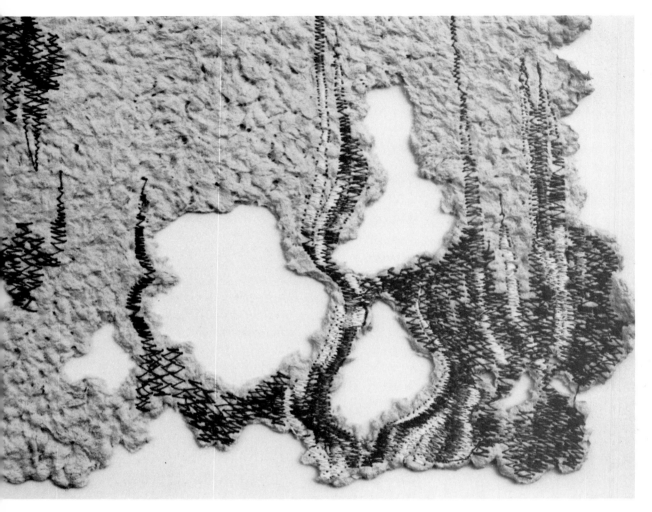

left when making the paper with a view to elaborating with stitchery; for example the paper could represent melting snow with small machine-embroidered plants or stones showing through. It is also possible to pleat or tuck translucent paper by machine to give denser areas.

These techniques could be used in a purely experimental and decorative way or applied to blinds.

Paper can blunt machine needles, though otherwise it should not do any harm to the machine; needles near the end of their lives could be used or a leather needle might be appropriate.

112 *A home-made paper with a rough texture will, surprisingly, take machine stitching quite readily. Bernina.*

113 *Heavy-duty plastic cut into a strip with one straight and one zigzag machine line down the centre, then tied in a simple knot which when flattened forms a pentagon. A series of these strips in different sizes could make a hanging or screen. Bernina.*

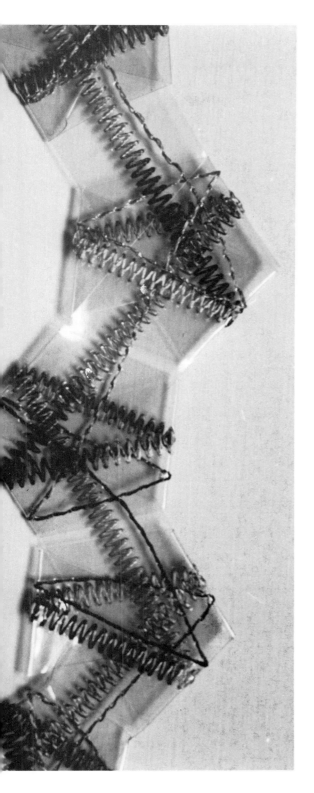

Plastic

One of the main drawbacks of plastic can be its impermanence, but if this is accepted, it is challenging material to work on.

Technically plastic can be difficult to feed through a machine so trials need to be made with different feet; Bernina suggest roller and teflon-coated feet; it is also possible to use the darning foot with the stiffer kind of clear plastic used for secondary forms of window glazing.

Because plastic is reversible different coloured threads can be used in top and bottom of the machine so that each side is the same but in a different colourway.

By placing layers of opaque fabric such as felt in between sheets of plastic, alternative dense and see-through areas are created. Transferring designs onto plastic can be a problem, so for a layered technique the following is a possible procedure:

1 Draw the design in outline on paper, deciding where areas of felt will be.

2 Transfer the relevant areas of design onto felt, and cut out.

3 Lay plastic, of window-glazing weight, on a flat surface.

4 Referring to the design, place pieces of felt in the correct position on the plastic.

5 Lay a second layer of plastic on top, taking care not to displace the felt. Static then holds all layers together so that machining can be worked either round or through the encapsulated felt.

By using snippets of thread or fabric rather than the solid mass of felt a more lively, mobile effect results.

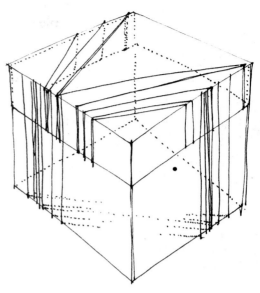

117 *A box made of transparent plastic; a student found that by working an open zigzag around the edges and oversewing through this stitching by hand, boxes and bags could readily be constructed. By making the lid or base in a simple cruciform, the minimum of construction was required. A feature could be made of straight or curved lines seen through from one side of the box to the other, or even a series of boxes within boxes. This could be extended to a major three-dimensional construction.*

ABOVE LEFT

114 *Broad strips of heavy-duty plastic with encapsulated bands of brightly coloured felts cut in varying widths to form a decorative hanging. Plastic rods were inserted to weight panels so that they hang straight. Bernina.*

115 *An enlargement of an area of an experimental panel based on plastic hexagons; in each hexagon, made from two layers of heavy-duty plastic, were contained snippets of a wide variety of threads and yarns, held in place with lines of straight stitching. Viking Husqvarna.* Alison Kirkby.

ABOVE

116 *An experimental plastic panel with areas of encapsulated felt in yellow, blue and green; partly colour-sprayed with car paint spray from the back to give an area of less bland texture. Bernina.*

13 From Design into Embroidery

'Design' is not such a fearsome word as it used to be: many more people are now prepared to attempt their own designs, albeit simple ones. Many people also now know that there are ways of designing other than putting a pencil to paper, and these techniques are helpful for beginners to gain confidence.

Photographs, particularly transparencies, which can be projected, are also a good basis for design, and if the embroiderer is willing to learn to draw, the design permutations are endless.

It must be remembered that designing and sketching are not the same process. *Sketching* is putting down on paper what the individual sees, that is factual evidence, as a 'source', the basis from which a synthesis of shapes and colours can be formed into an individual's view of the source. When designing, not all the detail need be included, or shapes may be transposed: in the simplest terms, a leaf may be added or subtracted from a stem, the size of a flower head exaggerated in proportion to a stem. *Interpretation* continues this process of synthesizing in fabric and thread, so that the final piece may bear little obvious relation to the original sketch. A design cannot be developed off the top of one's head, but must have some basis in fact, however tenuous, to be worthwhile. Information must be absorbed before it can go through the process of individual synthesizing and be expressed as a design. That is why it is important to choose something that interests you especially, and to try not to copy precisely a

design you have already seen worked, tempting though it may be, as it will come out as a watered down version of the original.

On the other hand, do not try too desperately to be 'original' as this rarely succeeds, but aim to be sincere about your subject and its interpretation and this will succeed. As a teacher in adult education I am often faced with a student saying 'I would like to do an embroidery like that one in the exhibition'; when they explain which piece it was, I realize it was by someone who took perhaps 20 years of trial and experience to reach that piece of work! Be ambitious but realistic as well.

Drawing

There often seems to be a misunderstanding in people's minds about drawing; because their teacher told them in the long ago past that they could not draw, they accept that premature judgement for the rest of their lives.

Drawing, in the context of collecting source material for design, means making a visual notebook of shapes and colours; this acts as a permanent reference to be used at any time,

118 *'Conversation Piece' is an amusing panel incorporating patchwork for the parrots and a mixture of hand and machine techniques forming the background.* Belinda Fairclough. Embroiderers' Guild Collection.

119 '*Fruits de Mer*': *a three-dimensional embroidery based on a platter of crustaceans. The prawns are chemical lace and the crab has back and claws in the same technique, mounted over brushed nylon for the crab body. Singer.* Carolyn Licence.

120 *A sketchbook page of views of an African marigold flower.*

which may be many years after the original drawing. This does not mean that the skill and talent of a Michelangelo are required, only the willingness to record in whatever medium the individual finds most acceptable, the images that have a personal appeal. Many people expect too much too early by way of facility and skill, but even if there is apparently no talent, with practice, training and persistence anyone can develop an individual visual record.

One of the best instructions I had from a drawing tutor was 'Look hard; do not draw what you think should be there, but draw what you see'. It is true that the mind can assume the shape goes thus and thus, but by looking hard and observing keenly you may see that the shape may not be what the mind assumes at all. One individual may see a shape quite differently to another; the great artist often shows us something familiar in a totally different light to our experience, thus making it unfamiliar and special.

There are many tools for drawing, so it is necessary to experiment in order to make a personal choice. The most obvious to try is pencil, but in the hand of the unpractised there is a great temptation to rub out, leading to constant alteration and finally despair. A felt-tip or metal-tip pen is often a better choice so that once the line is drawn there is no opportunity for alteration. Felt-tip pens can be bought cheaply and offer a wide range of thickness of tip, and colour variation.

Charcoal can help to prevent concentration on unnecessary detail as it is a bold medium. It also gives an interesting quality of line, going from thick to thin, and from light to dark depending on the pressure exerted. Charcoal does need to be fixed either with a patent fixative or even hair spray, or the drawing will blur.

Crayons, which are readily available, can be used to record colour or make colour notes; by overlaying different coloured crayons subtle colour mixes can be achieved which themselves suggest layering of fabric, or machining in a similar way with multi-coloured layers of thread. Pastels or paints require a little more

121 *A sketch of the overall appearance of the plant.*

122 *A drawing of a full-face flower.*

99

experience and skill for effective application and are useful for bolder areas of colour. Alternatively, colour photographs can be used as colour reference together with drawings.

For paper, an ordinary sketchbook is all that is necessary; it does help if it is a book, however small, as loose sheets easily get lost. Remember that the sketchbook is primarily for personal reference so that neatness and presentation are irrelevant, and content is the prime concern.

What to draw? This has to be an individual choice depending on inclination; many people find plants, whether garden or indoor, attractive subject matter and there is such a wealth of variation in leaf shape, plant structure and

flower form to choose from that it can never be exhausted. In sketching as in designing decisions have to be made. Should the flower be head-on, side view or three-quarters? How much of the plant to include? Within a limited frame or not? Which details need to be included to express the character of the plant? These are the questions that are unconsciously posed and have to be decided. It is wise to gather as much visual information together as possible, as even if it is not used immediately, a full sketchbook is the essential background to design.

Always aim to choose subjects that appeal to you and fill you with enthusiasm; the most effective embroidery is an individual and personal expression, and if you are enthusiastic about the subject matter it will be reflected in the finished work.

123 *Drawings of flowers in pots taken directly from life.*

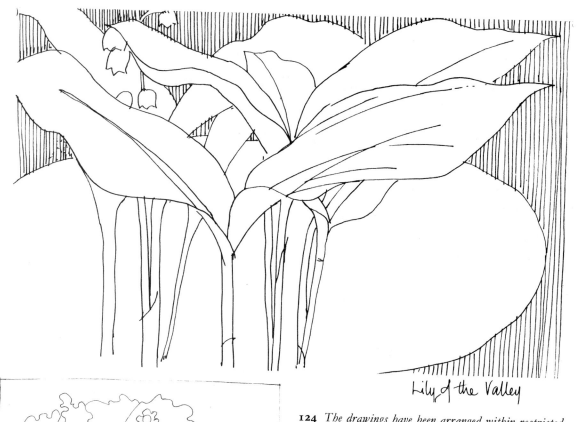

Lily of the Valley

124 *The drawings have been arranged within restricted frames and are so simplified that they can be used as they are as embroidery designs.*

125 *A free adaption of an African marigold suggesting areas of density for working on net, in layers of fabric or chemical lace, or directly onto georgette or organdie.*

The following ideas are merely suggestions for techniques of designing, many of which are not new but can be interpreted in a variety of ways. It is my experience that one of the most difficult leaps to make is from design (on paper) to embroidery; one design can be interpreted in a multitude of ways, depending on purpose and personal inclination.

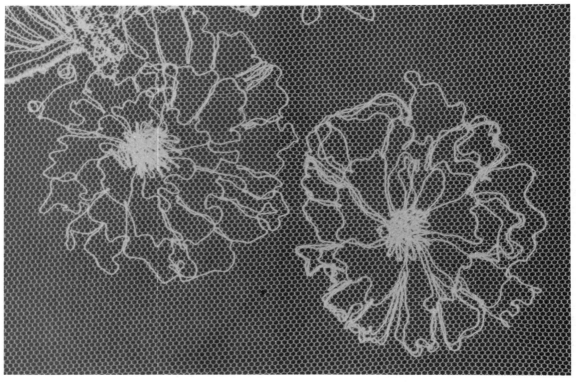

126 *Stages in interpretation of an African marigold:
the outline has been sketched with straight-stitch
machining onto net.*

BELOW
127 *Straight stitch with applied net.*

128 *A variation: more applied net and less straight
stitching.*

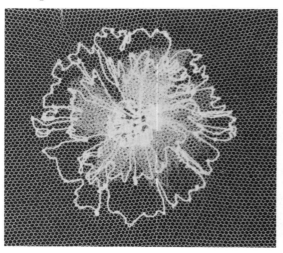

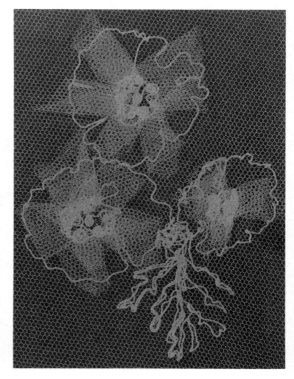

129 *The final piece shows flowers of varying sizes grouped together to form the decoration of a wedding veil.*

130 *The angle of the straw in the saucer in order to produce the best froth of bubbles from which to make a print.*

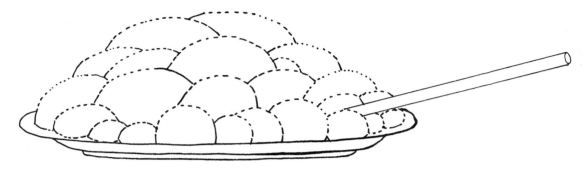

Bubble prints

Bubble prints can be an excellent design source as the whole or parts may be used for a variety of techniques. They are a form of accidental design.

Equipment needed:
a saucer
washing-up liquid
ink – any dark colour
water
drinking straws
typing paper or similar

1 Make a mixture of one part undiluted washing-up liquid, one part ink and two parts water; one part equals about half a fluid ounce in order to make a saucerful.

2 Mix all together thoroughly in a saucer.

3 Insert the straw in one side and blow until the liquid is frothy (**fig. 130**).

4 Quickly place the paper on top, leave for about five seconds and remove, and a print will result. Make several prints, and choose the best when they are dry.

This print may be placed under vanishing muslin or acetate fabric and the outline traced through (see page 15). Alternatively, a print may be made directly onto the fabric and allowed to dry before working.

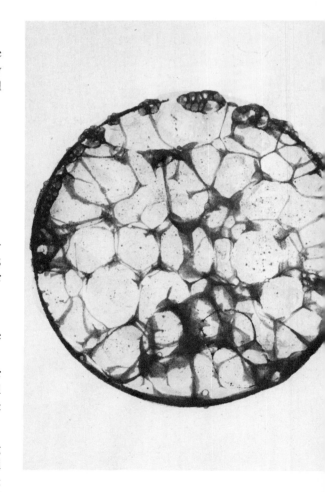

131 *A bubble print on paper.*

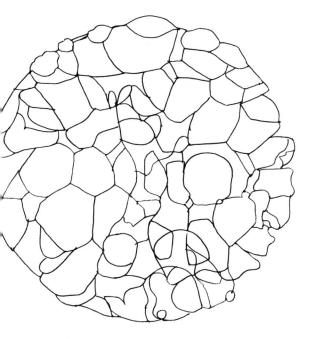

132 *Only the main outlines of the bubble print are traced, and they are suitable for working on vanishing muslin or in the acetone/acetate method if further connecting lines are added in the working.*

134 *The same flowers adapted for cutwork.*

133 *From the bubble-print tracing, limited areas are selected which form 'flowers' which could be filled with pulled thread textures or machined on net, incorporating different weights of thread.*

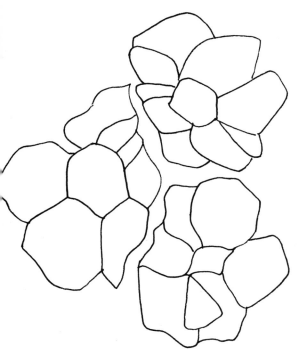

135 *An alternative bubble-print tracing showing its complexity of shapes; this could be the basis for layered fabrics, the darkened area suggesting a cut-away layer.*

136 *Sections traced from the edge of the bubble print, arranged to form a cutwork motif.*

OPPOSITE
137 *A scarf, the ends illustrating how a bubble print might be used. The 'lace' was worked on vanishing muslin in no. 50 sewing cotton in black to match the scarf, but small areas have appliqué of bronze and gunmetal lurex, and Madeira thread also enriches the lacy area.*

138 *Butterfly shapes and wing patterns, indicating the endless permutations of wing shape and decoration.*

Butterflies

These insects have always been a source of pleasure to me, although they may be considered over-familiar by some. Either go to a museum to study them or get a really informative book which shows plenty of detail. Make notes of overall shapes, colouring, and the incredible variation of pattern on the wings. This information may then be used as illustrated (**figs 138–44**).

139 *A border made from simplified butterfly shapes to form a collar.*

140 *A small butterfly sketched to suggest different interpretations even within this limited shape:*
(a) layered fabrics
(b) one of the chemical lace techniques
(c) cutwork.

141 *Another border formed from a butterfly wing, which could form an edge to a variety of items such as a handkerchief, sleeve, skirt or cushion.*

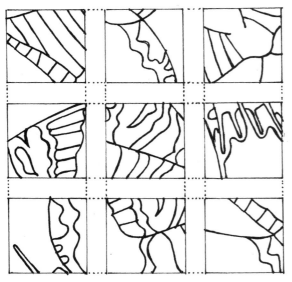

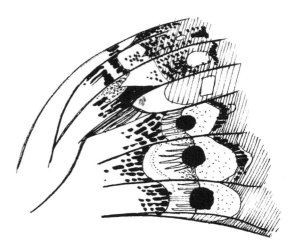

142 *Abstracted sections of a butterfly wing pattern which could form the basis, much enlarged, of a hanging in plastic, cutwork or layering, or a mixture of all three.*

ABOVE RIGHT
143 *The variety of texture observed in a butterfly wing which would translate well into machine embroidery on see-through fabric, using different weights of thread, different widths of zigzag, cable stitch and whip stitch.*

144 *Cut a butterfly outline in two sizes several times over from paper, lay on a background and arrange in a group; the design can then be interpreted in net appliqué, layered fabrics or cutwork.*

Reflections

All about us every day are designs waiting to be seen, if only we can train ourselves to see them. Reflections are so familiar they may easily be overlooked. They can be found in pots and pans and crumpled cooking foil, in car mirrors, hub caps and bumpers, on wet pavements, on dark winter evenings, on rivers or puddles and in shop windows and especially nowadays in tower blocks where glass covers almost the whole surface. One of the most interesting series of abstract shapes I have seen was a row of socks on a hanging drier reflected in a double-glazed window on a dark evening!

For reflections in tower blocks, a camera can be most useful; take several shots from different angles and at different distances from the building, if this is practicable, and does not involve standing in the middle of a busy street! If you take colour transparencies these can be projected directly onto paper and the outlines drawn in; you will be developing your individuality in deciding just which lines to include. Designing is largely decision making, and no one can do it but yourself. Even pointing the camera at a selected area is making a decision about which related shapes you think look well together. To see how the shapes may be used see page 112.

146 Distorted reflections in a glass-faced building.

145 A sketchbook page of distorted reflections in the glass windows of a tower block; this drawing was made while a coachload of ladies gathered to begin a day's outing and nobody paid the slightest attention!

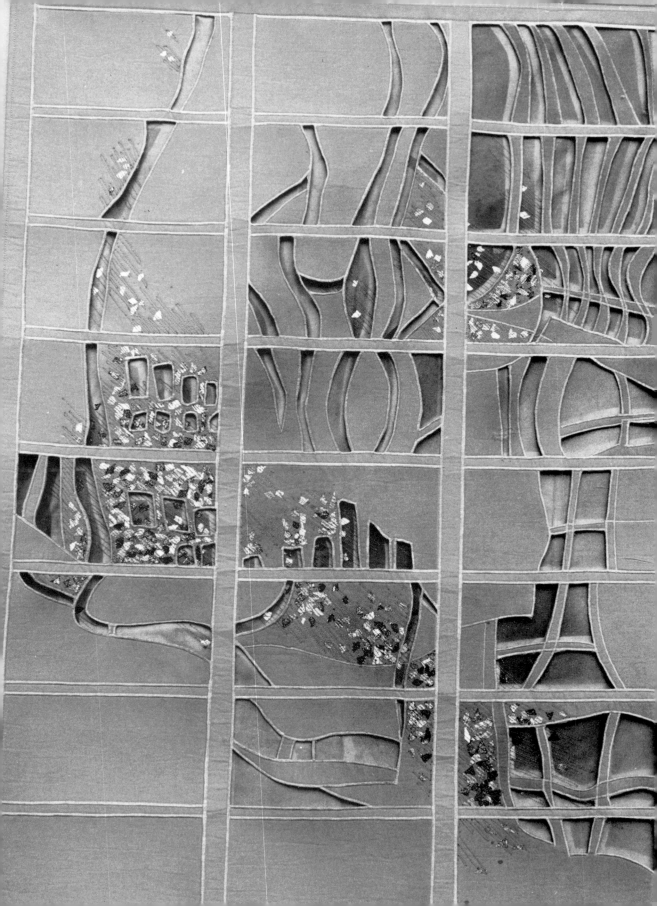

147 *'Reflections': a panel based on shapes seen in a glass-faced tower block, which have been inverted. The surface is cotton poplin bonded onto pelmet vilene, which was then cutworked and snippets of twinkly fabric were appliquéd onto selected areas. The backing is free-hanging and is spray-painted and applied. The overall size of the panel is 1 metre (39 in.) by 66 cm (26 in.) and the cutwork took over 1300 metres (1420 yards) of thread. Elna and Bernina.*

Interpretation

Interpretation often seems to stump people because a jump has to be made from paper to fabric. How is it made? The only answer is by doing it, physically. There is a temptation to try to think it through as a series of mental impressions, but the only way of finding solutions is to start applying needle to fabric and what will succeed or not immediately becomes apparent.

After drawing an outline design and roughly sketching in tone, I prefer to work a series of trial runs, on different fabrics or in different techniques, each growing from its predecessor until I find a solution that seems satisfactory. This may sound time-consuming but in my experience it saves time eventually and gives a clearer direction of how to tackle the finished piece. This does not mean that once the decision has been made to start on the main piece all problems have been solved; it is still necessary to think continuously through an embroidery, being constantly willing to adjust and rethink to achieve a successful embroidery.

148 *Drawing of an end-of-season tomato plant.* Pamela Warner.

149 *Interpretation of a tomato plant; the tomatoes are in padded panne velvet, with wrapped stems and leaves in machined organdie.* Pamela Warner.

113

This system of interpretation is only one of many alternatives. Some embroiderers like to design their work entirely on paper, as a cartoon, and then copy this onto fabric; others start directly onto fabric from only a sketched or sketchy idea, building it up bit by bit as they go. Only by being willing to try different ways of interpreting will the individual find what suits him or her. There is no guaranteed path to success and achievement for the designer/craftsman, because the essence of their work is individuality.

150 *'Two Figures with a Frog': the mysterious, fairytale quality of this work is based on objects collected and drawn 'aiming to evoke images through the strange relationship of figures and personal objects'. It is worked in machine embroidery on organdie in a variety of threads, the female figure being chemical lace. Bernina. Alison Edwards.*

Suppliers

UK

At the time of going to press the following suppliers are trading, but always check before sending orders or money that the addresses are still valid and that they stock the goods listed.

Mary Allen
Wirksworth
Derbyshire DE4 4BN

Full range of DMC machine threads.

Borovick Fabrics Ltd
16 Berwick Street
London W1

Wide range of fabrics including transparent and see-through.

John Lewis
Oxford Street
London W1

Large range of sewing threads; machine needles and accessories; wide range of fabrics and interlinings.

Liberty
Regent Street
London W1

Lawn and high quality cotton fabrics are included in their range of good quality fabrics of all sorts.

MacCulloch & Wallis Ltd
25–6 Dering Street
London W1R OBH

Vanishing muslin; 'stitch-and-tear'; large spools of sewing thread; machine needles; circular frames; acetate fabric.

Silken Strands
33 Linksway
Gatley
Cheadle
Cheshire SK8 4LA

Madeira metallic threads; Natesh threads (including Titania).

Whaleys (Bradford) Ltd
Harris Court
Great Horton
Bradford
West Yorkshire BD7 4EQ

Water-soluble fabric, vanishing muslin and many other fabrics (minimum order requirement).

For addresses of retailers of DMC threads in Great Britain apply to:

Dunlicraft Ltd
Pullman Road
Wigston
Leicestershire LE8 2DY

For addresses of retailers of Anchor embroidery threads in Great Britain apply to:

J & P Coats (UK) Ltd
Harlequin Avenue
Great West Road
Brentford
Middlesex

or Coats Domestic Marketing Division
39 Durham Street
Glasgow G41 1BS

USA

Appleton Brothers of London
West Main Road
Little Compton
Rhode Island 02837

American Thread Corporation
90 Park Avenue
New York

Threadbenders
2260 Como Avenue
St Paul
Minnesota 55108

The Thread Shed
307 Freeport Road
Pittsburgh
Pennsylvania 15215

Sewing Machine Manufacturers

UK

Bernina Sewing Machines
Bogod House
50–2 Great Sutton Street
London EC1V 0DJ

Elna Sewing Machines (GB) Ltd
180–2 Tottenham Court Road
London W1P 9LE

Frister and Rossman Sewing Machines Ltd
Mark Way
Swanley
Kent BR8 8NQ

Jones Sewing Machine Co. Ltd
Shepley Street
Guide Bridge
Audenshaw
Manchester M34 5JD
Jones and Brother machines

Knitmaster Ltd
39–45 Cowleaze Road
Kingston-upon-Thames
Surrey KT2 6DT

Necchi Sewing Machines
Diana House
97 Hoxton Street
London N1

New Home Sewing Machine Co. Ltd
Cromwell Road
Bredbury
Stockport
Cheshire SK6 2SH

The Singer Company (UK)
255 High Street
Guildford
Surrey GU1 3DH

Toyota Sewing and Knitting (Aisin (UK) Ltd)
34 High Street
Bromley
Kent

Viking-Husqvarna Ltd
PO Box 10
Oakley Road
Luton LU4 9QW

USA

Larson Bernina Corporation
2017 East 78 Street
Minneapolis 55401

White Sewing Machine Co.
11750 Berea Road
Cleveland
Ohio 44111
Elna machines

The Singer Company
8 Stamford Forum
Stamford
Connecticut 06904

Bibliography

Bain, George, *Celtic Art*, Constable 1977

Benson, Dorothy, *Your Machine Embroidery*,
  Sylvan Press 1952

Campbell-Harding, Valerie, *Faces and Figures in
  Embroidery*, Batsford 1979 & 1985

Churchill-Bath, Virginia, *Lace*, Studio Vista 1974

Clucas, Joy, *Your Machine for Embroidery*, Bell
  1975

Coleman, Anne, *The Creative Sewing Machine*,
  Batsford 1979 & 1981

Head, Carol, *Old Sewing Machines*, Shire
  Publications 1982

Lemon, Jane, *Embroidered Boxes*, Batsford 1984

Messent, Jan, *Embroidery and Animals*, Batsford
  1984

O'Brien, James F., *Design by Accident*, Dover
  1969

Risley, Christine, *Machine Embroidery*, Studio
  Vista 1973

Watson, Allan, and Whalley, Paul, *Butterflies and
  Moths in Colour*, Peerage Books 1975 & 1983

Index

Numbers in *italic* refer to the figure numbers of the illustrations